MW00931604

500 Careers and Salaries

The Job Seeker's Atlas. Salaries and Roles Across Industries

— 2025 edition —

Thank you!

We dedicated many hours to compiling this information for you. This is the book we would have loved having during our teen years and later on when we switched careers.

If you find this career guide useful, please consider leaving a review on Amazon. We'd love to hear from you!

You can use this QR code to submit your review

Table Of Contents

9

The U.S. Department of Labor is the source for Salary (median) and Degree Level Required.

The **median** salary is the value that separates the higher half of a salary range from the lower half. In other words, if you were to arrange all the salaries in a list from the lowest to the highest, the median salary would be the middle number. If there is an even number of salaries in the list, the median is found by taking the average of the two middle numbers.

In contrast to the average (or mean) salary, which sums all salaries and divides by the number of salaries, the median is often a more accurate reflection of the typical income within a group because it is not skewed by extremely high or low salaries. If a CEO earns a very high salary, for example, that could raise the average significantly, but the median would remain a better indicator of what a "typical" employee might earn.

Accountants

Aspect	Detail
Hourly Rate	$38.50
Annual Salary	$80,000
Degree Level Required	Bachelor's degree

They prepare and maintain financial records for businesses and individuals. They ensure that financial records are accurate and complete, and they comply with all applicable laws and regulations. Accountants may also prepare tax returns, analyze financial data, and provide financial advice.

Auditors

Aspect	Detail
Hourly Rate	$38.50
Annual Salary	$80,000
Degree Level Required	Bachelor's degree

They are responsible for independently reviewing and verifying the accuracy of financial records. They work to ensure that financial statements are free from material misstatements and that they comply with accounting standards. Auditors may also provide recommendations for improving financial controls and internal processes.

Actuaries

Aspect	Detail
Hourly Rate	$57.70
Annual Salary	$120,000
Degree Level Required	Bachelor's degree

They use mathematical and statistical methods to assess risks and uncertainties. They are employed by insurance companies, pension funds, and other financial institutions to develop insurance products, pricing, and risk management strategies. Actuaries also play a role in the development of social security and other government programs.

Acupuncturists

Aspect	Detail
Hourly Rate	$37.6
Annual Salary	$78,300
Degree Level Required	Master's degree

They are practitioners of a traditional Chinese medicine technique utilizing the insertion of thin needles at specific points of the body. They aim to improve energy flow (qi) and restore balance to promote healing and pain reduction. Acupuncturists address a variety of ailments including chronic pain, stress/anxiety, headaches, digestive issues, and more.

Adhesive Bonding Machine Operators and Tenders

Aspect	Detail
Hourly Rate	$21
Annual Salary	$43,600
Degree Level Required	High school diploma or equivalent

They work in manufacturing settings to join materials together using specialized equipment. Their responsibilities include setting up and operating bonding machines based on product specifications, applying adhesives and preparing materials for bonding, monitoring the bonding process to ensure quality and adherence, and performing routine maintenance and troubleshooting on machines.

Administrative Law Judges, Adjudicators, and Hearing Officers

Aspect	Detail
Hourly Rate	$53.4
Annual Salary	$111,100
Degree Level Required	Doctoral or professional degree

They oversee and direct the supportive services of an organization. They ensure that the physical environment and services, such as recordkeeping, mail distribution, and office upkeep, run smoothly and efficiently. These managers may also oversee facilities planning, maintenance, and custodial operations. Their role is pivotal in ensuring that the workplace meets the needs of employees and conforms to health and safety standards. They work closely with upper management to align the administrative services with the strategic goals of the organization.

Administrative Services Managers

Aspect	Detail
Hourly Rate	$51.2
Annual Salary	$106,500
Degree Level Required	Bachelor's degree

They provide instruction to adults in a variety of subjects, including reading, writing, and mathematics, aiming to improve their basic skills or attain a high school equivalency credential. They may also teach English as a Second Language (ESL) to non-native speakers. These educators assess students' educational levels, develop instructional materials, and employ various teaching methods to meet the diverse needs of adult learners. Their work is vital in helping adults achieve personal, educational, and professional goals, contributing to lifelong learning and empowerment.

Adult Basic & Secondary Education

Aspect	Detail
Hourly Rate	$29.1
Annual Salary	$60,600
Degree Level Required	Bachelor's degree

They plan and direct programs to generate interest in products or services. They work with art directors, sales agents, and financial staff members to create compelling advertising campaigns that reach target audiences through various media. These managers negotiate contracts, develop pricing strategies, and analyze the effectiveness of advertising campaigns to adjust strategies as necessary. Their creativity and strategic thinking drive the success of marketing efforts, aiming to increase sales and market share for their company or clients.

Advertising and Promotions Managers

Aspect	Detail
Hourly Rate	$63.4
Annual Salary	$131,900
Degree Level Required	Bachelor's degree

They also known as account executives or sales representatives, sell advertising space or time. They work for media companies, including newspapers, magazines, websites, and broadcast stations, and communicate with businesses and individuals to sell advertising space or airtime. These agents must understand their clients' advertising needs and propose suitable advertising packages to meet these needs. They also prepare and present sales presentations, negotiate contracts, and maintain client relationships. Their success is measured by their ability to meet sales targets and generate revenue for their media outlet.

Advertising Sales Agents

Aspect	Detail
Hourly Rate	$29.5
Annual Salary	$61,300
Degree Level Required	High school diploma or equivalent

They design, develop, and test aircraft, spacecraft, and missiles, as well as supervise the manufacture of these products. They apply principles of physics and mathematics to solve problems in the design, development, and testing of the durability and safety of aerospace products. Aerospace engineers may specialize in areas such as structural design, navigation systems, or propulsion systems. Their work is critical in advancing technology for aviation, defense, and space exploration, ensuring the functionality and safety of flight and space vehicles.

Aerospace Engineers

Aspect	Detail
Hourly Rate	$62.90
Annual Salary	$130,800
Degree Level Required	Bachelor's degree

They are involved in the design, analysis, and testing of airborne and space vehicles, including planes, helicopters, rockets, and satellites. They utilize advanced knowledge in aerodynamics, avionics, propulsion, and materials science to create vehicles that safely operate in the Earth's atmosphere and beyond. These engineers must consider numerous factors such as fuel efficiency, environmental impact, safety, and cost. They often specialize in specific areas like structural design, guidance systems, or production methods and may work on projects ranging from commercial aircraft design to military defense systems and space exploration missions.

Agents of Artists, Performers, and Athletes

Aspect	Detail
Hourly Rate	$40.8
Annual Salary	$84,900
Degree Level Required	Bachelor's degree

They work as intermediaries between their clients and potential employers or sponsors. They negotiate contracts, arrange meetings, and promote the talents of artists, performers, and athletes to secure employment and endorsement deals. These agents must have a deep understanding of the entertainment, sports, and arts industries, including current market trends and legal considerations. Their effectiveness is measured by their ability to secure lucrative and career-advancing opportunities for their clients, balancing the interests and well-being of the artist or athlete with the demands of the industry.

Agricultural Engineers

Aspect	Detail
Hourly Rate	$42.7
Annual Salary	$88,800
Degree Level Required	Bachelor's degree

They apply engineering principles and technologies to the agricultural sector to solve problems related to sustainable agricultural production. They may work on a variety of projects, including designing farm machinery and equipment, developing water irrigation systems, and creating efficient crop storage solutions. These engineers aim to increase the efficiency and environmental sustainability of agricultural practices, ensuring food security and safety while minimizing environmental impacts. Their work involves close collaboration with the agricultural community to implement solutions that are both technologically advanced and practical for farmers.

Agricultural Equipment Operators

Aspect	Detail
Hourly Rate	$19.1
Annual Salary	$39,700
Degree Level Required	No formal educational credential

They are responsible for operating and maintaining the heavy machinery used in the cultivation, harvesting, and processing of crops. This includes tractors, combines, plows, and irrigation equipment. These operators must understand the workings of the machines they handle and perform basic maintenance to ensure operational efficiency. Their role is crucial in modern farming operations, enabling large-scale production with efficiency and precision. Safety and adaptability are key aspects of their job, as they must navigate varying field conditions and operate complex machinery effectively.

Agricultural Inspectors

Aspect	Detail
Hourly Rate	$23.1
Annual Salary	$48,100
Degree Level Required	Bachelor's degree

They ensure compliance with laws and regulations regarding the safety and quality of agricultural products. They inspect crops, livestock, and processing facilities to enforce government standards related to health, safety, and environmental protection. These inspectors may collect samples for analysis, check for pests or diseases, and verify that agricultural practices meet regulatory standards. Their work is essential in protecting public health by ensuring that the agricultural products reaching the market are safe to consume and that agricultural operations do not harm the environment.

Agricultural Technicians

Aspect	Detail
Hourly Rate	$20.8
Annual Salary	$43,200
Degree Level Required	Associate's degree

They work closely with agricultural scientists to improve farming efficiency and product quality. They assist in research, the development of new agricultural methods, and the monitoring of environmental and crop conditions. Their duties may include setting up experiments, collecting data, and analyzing soil and water samples. Technicians play a critical role in implementing technological advances in agriculture, such as precision farming techniques, and contribute to the development of sustainable farming practices that can lead to higher yields and reduced environmental impact.

Air Traffic Controllers

Aspect	Detail
Hourly Rate	$66.1
Annual Salary	$137,400
Degree Level Required	Associate's degree

They are responsible for the safe and efficient movement of aircraft in the sky and on the ground. They manage the flow of airplanes through controlled airspace and on the airport's runways and taxiways. Using radar, radio communications, and other navigation systems, they provide pilots with instructions to ensure safe distances between aircraft, efficient routing, and timely takeoffs and landings. Their role is critical in preventing collisions and minimizing delays, requiring intense concentration, quick decision-making, and the ability to manage complex situations under pressure.

Aircraft Cargo Handling Supervisors

Aspect	Detail
Hourly Rate	$28.4
Annual Salary	$59,000
Degree Level Required	High school diploma or equivalent

They oversee the loading, unloading, and securing of cargo on aircraft. They determine the weight and distribution of cargo to ensure safe aircraft balance. These supervisors direct ground crews, train new employees, and may even accompany cargo in-flight to monitor its handling.

Aircraft Mechanics and Service Technicians

Aspect	Detail
Hourly Rate	$36.1
Annual Salary	$75,100
Degree Level Required	Postsecondary non-degree award

They are responsible for inspecting, maintaining, and repairing aircraft. They troubleshoot issues with engines, airframes, hydraulics, and other aircraft systems. These professionals ensure aircraft are airworthy and adhere to strict safety regulations.

Aircraft Service Attendants

Aspect	Detail
Hourly Rate	$18.8
Annual Salary	$39,200
Degree Level Required	High school diploma or equivalent

They work to clean and prepare aircraft interiors between flights. They tasks include restocking supplies, cleaning seats and surfaces, removing trash, and sometimes de-icing aircraft exteriors. Service attendants ensure aircraft cabins are clean and ready for passengers.

Aircraft Structure, Surfaces, and Systems Assemblers

Aspect	Detail
Hourly Rate	$29.5
Annual Salary	$61,300
Degree Level Required	High school diploma or equivalent

They build aircraft components and systems according to detailed specifications and blueprints. They work with sheet metal, composites, wiring, and other materials to construct parts of the aircraft fuselage, wings, control surfaces, and interior systems.

Airfield Operations Specialists

Aspect	Detail
Hourly Rate	$24.6
Annual Salary	$51,200
Degree Level Required	High school diploma or equivalent

They coordinate activities on the ground at airports to ensure safe and efficient aircraft operations. They communicate with pilots, direct ground traffic, manage runways and taxiways, and respond to emergencies. These specialists play a vital role in airport safety.

Airline Pilots, Copilots, and Flight Engineers

Aspect	Detail
Hourly Rate	$105.4
Annual Salary	$219,200
Degree Level Required	Bachelor's degree

They are responsible for operating and navigating commercial aircraft. Airline pilots command the aircraft, while copilots, also known as first officers, share in the operation and monitoring of the flight. Flight engineers assist in the operation of the aircraft systems and may conduct pre-flight inspections. These professionals must have a deep knowledge of aviation principles, strong communication skills, and the ability to respond to emergency situations.

Ambulance Drivers

Aspect	Detail
Hourly Rate	$15.7
Annual Salary	$32,600
Degree Level Required	High school diploma or equivalent

They have the vital role of transporting patients to healthcare facilities in emergency situations. They must drive with speed and efficiency while ensuring the safety and comfort of the patient. Knowledge of first aid and life support is often necessary, as they may assist paramedics in providing care. They also need to maintain ambulance equipment and keep accurate patient records.

Amusement and Recreation Attendants

Aspect	Detail
Hourly Rate	$14.1
Annual Salary	$29,400
Degree Level Required	No formal educational credential

They operate attractions, assist with the organization of recreational activities, and maintain the safety and cleanliness of the facility. They interact directly with guests, providing service with a friendly demeanor, and handle transactions for tickets or concessions. Their primary goal is to enhance the guest experience while ensuring a safe environment.

Anesthesiologists

Aspect	Detail
Hourly Rate	$142.50
Annual Salary	$296,400
Degree Level Required	Doctoral or professional degree

They are physicians specializing in perioperative care, developing anesthetic plans, and the administration of anesthetics. They are responsible for the safety and pain management of patients undergoing surgery. Preoperative evaluation of patients, determining anesthetics appropriate for patients based on medical history, and monitoring patients' vital signs during surgical procedures are some of their primary responsibilities.

Animal Breeders

Aspect	Detail
Hourly Rate	$22.9
Annual Salary	$47,600
Degree Level Required	High school diploma or equivalent

They apply their knowledge of genetics and animal science to manage the mating and reproduction of animals. They select and breed animals according to characteristics and standards, and may also oversee the care of pregnant females. Their work can range from domestic pets to livestock and may involve keeping detailed records of breeding, births, and other aspects of animal husbandry.

Animal Caretakers

Aspect	Detail
Hourly Rate	$15
Annual Salary	$31,200
Degree Level Required	High school diploma or equivalent

They look after animals in various settings, such as kennels, zoos, stables, animal shelters, pet stores, and aquariums. They feed, groom, and exercise animals, and may also administer medications or clean living spaces. They provide both the physical and emotional needs of animals in their care.

Animal Control Workers

Aspect	Detail
Hourly Rate	$20.8
Annual Salary	$43,200
Degree Level Required	High school diploma or equivalent

They help ensure public safety by handling animals that may be lost, abandoned, injured, or dangerous. They respond to calls about stray or aggressive animals, investigate cases of animal cruelty, rescue injured animals, and occasionally provide care until the animals can be returned to their owners or placed in a shelter.

Animal Scientists

Aspect	Detail
Hourly Rate	$33.8
Annual Salary	$70,200
Degree Level Required	Bachelor's degree

They study the biology and management of animals that are under human control, primarily livestock species. Their research aims to improve the efficiency, health, and welfare of these animals through advancements in nutrition, genetics, reproduction, and housing.

Animal Trainers

Aspect	Detail
Hourly Rate	$18.7
Annual Salary	$38,900
Degree Level Required	High school diploma or equivalent

They work with animals to teach them specific responses to commands for a variety of purposes, including obedience, performance, riding, security, or assisting people with disabilities. They use various training techniques to modify animal behavior and must be patient and consistent in their methods. They also often educate the animal's owner on how to maintain and reinforce the training.

Anthropologists and Archeologists

Aspect	Detail
Hourly Rate	$30.7
Annual Salary	$63,800
Degree Level Required	Master's degree

They study human societies and cultures, both past and present. They analyze social structures, language, beliefs, and material remains.

Archeologists specifically focus on recovering and interpreting artifacts and physical evidence from past civilizations to understand human history.

Arbitrators, Mediators, and Conciliators

Aspect	Detail
Hourly Rate	$34.4
Annual Salary	$71,600
Degree Level Required	Bachelor's degree

They help resolve disputes outside of court. Arbitrators issue binding decisions after hearing all sides of a case. Mediators facilitate negotiations between parties to help them reach a mutually agreeable solution. Conciliators work to informally improve communication and lessen hostility in a dispute.

Architects, Except Landscape and Naval

Aspect	Detail
Hourly Rate	$44.9
Annual Salary	$93,400
Degree Level Required	Bachelor's degree

They design buildings and other structures. They combine function, aesthetics, and safety to create spaces that are practical and visually appealing. Architects oversee the planning, development of blueprints, and often the construction process of a structure.

Architectural and Engineering Managers

Aspect	Detail
Hourly Rate	$79.5
Annual Salary	$165,400
Degree Level Required	Bachelor's degree

They plan, direct, and coordinate activities within architectural and engineering firms. They manage projects, budgets, staff, and the overall technical direction of their organizations.

Architecture Teachers, Postsecondary

Aspect	Detail
Hourly Rate	$50.9
Annual Salary	$105,800
Degree Level Required	Doctoral or professional degree

They teach courses in architecture at colleges and universities. They instruct students on design theory, architectural history, construction methods, and professional practices within the field of architecture.

Archivists

Aspect	Detail
Hourly Rate	$28.8
Annual Salary	$60,000
Degree Level Required	Master's degree

They collect, organize, and preserve historically valuable materials such as documents, photographs, and artifacts. They appraise, catalog, and make these materials accessible to researchers and the public.

Art Directors

Aspect	Detail
Hourly Rate	$51.2
Annual Salary	$106,500
Degree Level Required	Bachelor's degree

They are responsible for the overall visual style of publications, advertisements, movies, or television productions. They determine the artistic direction, collaborate with photographers, illustrators, and other designers to realize their vision.

Astronomers

Aspect	Detail
Hourly Rate	$61.5
Annual Salary	$128,000
Degree Level Required	Doctoral or professional degree

They study the universe, including stars, planets, galaxies, and other celestial objects. Using telescopes, satellites, and complex analysis, they research the origins, physical properties, and evolution of the universe.

Athletes and Sports Competitors

Aspect	Detail
Hourly Rate	$33.8
Annual Salary	$70,280
Degree Level Required	No formal educational credential

They engage in organized, officiated sporting events to entertain spectators. They maintain peak physical condition, practice their sport, and study their opponents to optimize performance. Athletes must understand the rules and strategies of their sport, often dedicating a significant portion of their lives to training, while competitors participate in professional, amateur, or collegiate sports.

Athletic Trainers

Aspect	Detail
Hourly Rate	$27.9
Annual Salary	$58,000
Degree Level Required	Master's degree

They specialize in preventing, diagnosing, and treating muscle and bone injuries and illnesses. They work with people of all ages and skill levels, from young children to professional athletes. Athletic trainers provide vital care during athletic events, develop injury prevention programs, and if injuries occur, they apply emergency care or first aid.

Atmospheric and Space Scientists

Aspect	Detail
Hourly Rate	$44.7
Annual Salary	$92,900
Degree Level Required	Bachelor's degree

They investigate the scientific phenomena of the earth's atmosphere and beyond. They might focus on weather patterns, environmental changes, or space exploration. These scientists use sophisticated technology to predict the weather and climate trends, or to conduct research on the atmosphere's characteristics.

Audio and Video Technicians

Aspect	Detail
Hourly Rate	$24.90
Annual Salary	$51,700
Degree Level Required	Postsecondary non-degree award

They set up and operate the electronic equipment used to record, broadcast, and edit sound and video for various events and productions. They may work on live events, such as concerts and conferences, or in post-production for film and television.

Audiologists

Aspect	Detail
Hourly Rate	$42.2
Annual Salary	$87,800
Degree Level Required	Doctoral or professional degree

They are healthcare professionals specializing in identifying, diagnosing, treating, and monitoring disorders of the auditory and vestibular system portions of the ear. They are equipped to deal with hearing loss and balance disorders, fit and dispense hearing aids, and advise on hearing conservation.

Audiovisual Equipment Installers and Repairers

Aspect	Detail
Hourly Rate	$23.3
Annual Salary	$48,400
Degree Level Required	Postsecondary non-degree award

They focus on the installation, maintenance, and repair of audio and video equipment. This includes equipment in homes, offices, schools, and a range of other institutions. They must understand electronic systems and be able to troubleshoot problems that arise with these technologies.

Automotive Body and Related Repairers

Aspect	Detail
Hourly Rate	$23.50
Annual Salary	$48,800
Degree Level Required	High school diploma or equivalent

They restore, refinish, and replace vehicle bodies and frames. They assess collision damage and perform repairs, often working with a variety of tools and materials. Their work can range from simple dents to realigning damaged car frames.

Automotive Glass Installers and Repairers

Aspect	Detail
Hourly Rate	$21.8
Annual Salary	$45,400
Degree Level Required	High school diploma or equivalent

They replace or repair broken windshields and window glass in motor vehicles. They must carefully remove damaged glass without causing further damage, then install new glass ensuring a perfect fit and waterproof seal.

Automotive Service Technicians and Mechanics

Aspect	Detail
Hourly Rate	$23
Annual Salary	$47,800
Degree Level Required	Postsecondary non-degree award

They inspect, maintain, and repair cars and light trucks. They must understand the complex systems in vehicles, use diagnostic tools to identify issues, and perform necessary repairs or maintenance. They also provide advice on vehicle care and upkeep to customers.

Avionics Technicians

Aspect	Detail
Hourly Rate	$37.3
Annual Salary	$77,500
Degree Level Required	Associate's degree

They are specialized technicians who repair and maintain the electronic systems on an aircraft, such as radio communication, aircraft navigation, and flight control systems. They must precisely follow federal regulations and use a variety of diagnostic devices to troubleshoot and fix issues.

Baggage Porters and Bellhops

Aspect	Detail
Hourly Rate	$16.8
Annual Salary	$34,900
Degree Level Required	High school diploma or equivalent

They assist guests at hotels and other travel accommodations with their luggage and other belongings. They carry bags, provide directions, and may offer other services like room tours and recommendations on local amenities.

Bakers

Aspect	Detail
Hourly Rate	$16.8
Annual Salary	$35,000
Degree Level Required	No formal educational credential

They mix, prepare, and bake a variety of bread, pastries, cakes, and other baked goods. They work in bakeries, restaurants, and grocery stores ensuring the quality and freshness of baked products. Bakers follow recipes, measure ingredients, and operate ovens and other baking equipment.

Barbers

Aspect	Detail
Hourly Rate	$17.4
Annual Salary	$36,200
Degree Level Required	Postsecondary non-degree award

They provide hair care services to clients, primarily men. They cut, trim, shampoo, and style hair. Barbers may also shave and shape facial hair.

Bartenders

Aspect	Detail
Hourly Rate	$15.2
Annual Salary	$31,600
Degree Level Required	No formal educational credential

They prepare and serve alcoholic and non-alcoholic beverages to customers in bars and restaurants. They mix drinks according to recipes, take orders, manage bar inventory, and often collect payments. Bartenders need knowledge of drink recipes and responsible alcohol service practices.

Bicycle Repairers

Aspect	Detail
Hourly Rate	$18.5
Annual Salary	$38,400
Degree Level Required	High school diploma or equivalent

They diagnose, adjust, repair, and maintain bicycles. They fix flat tires, replace worn parts, adjust brakes and gears, and ensure bikes are safe and in good riding condition.

Bill and Account Collectors

Aspect	Detail
Hourly Rate	$21.3
Annual Salary	$44,300
Degree Level Required	High school diploma or equivalent

They contact individuals and businesses who have overdue payments. They negotiate payment plans, track payments, and may initiate further collection actions if necessary.

Billing and Posting Clerks

Aspect	Detail
Hourly Rate	$21.9
Annual Salary	$45,600
Degree Level Required	High school diploma or equivalent

They compile, process, and maintain billing records for customers or patients. They calculate charges, prepare invoices, update account information, and may answer questions about bills.

Biochemists and Biophysicists

Aspect	Detail
Hourly Rate	$51.7
Annual Salary	$107,500
Degree Level Required	Doctoral or professional degree

They study the chemical and physical principles of living things and of biological processes. They conduct complex research projects and experiments to understand the mechanics of life at a molecular level, often aiming to develop new technologies and solutions in fields like medicine and environmental science.

Bioengineers and Biomedical Engineers

Aspect	Detail
Hourly Rate	$48.5
Annual Salary	$100,800
Degree Level Required	Bachelor's degree

They combine the principles of biology and engineering to create products and technologies that improve the health and medical fields. They develop medical devices, equipment, computer systems, and software used in healthcare. Their work includes research and development of artificial organs, prostheses, instrumentation, medical information systems, and health management and care delivery systems.

Bookkeeping, Accounting, and Auditing Clerks

Aspect	Detail
Hourly Rate	$22.8
Annual Salary	$47,500
Degree Level Required	Some college, no degree

They play a crucial role in the financial upkeep of businesses. They record financial transactions, update statements, and check financial records for accuracy. Their duties encompass a wide range of bookkeeping and accounting tasks, including balancing accounts and ensuring financial records are complete and correct.

Brickmasons and Blockmasons

Aspect	Detail
Hourly Rate	$28.7
Annual Salary	$59,700
Degree Level Required	High school diploma or equivalent

They are skilled tradespeople who lay and bind building materials, such as brick, structural tile, concrete block, cinder block, glass block, and terra-cotta block, with mortar and other substances to construct or repair walls, partitions, arches, sewers, and other structures.

Broadcast Technicians

Aspect	Detail
Hourly Rate	$27.7
Annual Salary	$57,700
Degree Level Required	Associate's degree

They set up, operate, and maintain the electrical equipment for radio programs, television broadcasts, concerts, sound recordings, and movies. They ensure that sound and visuals are clear and synchronized, working in various locations such as studios, sporting arenas, or theaters.

Brokerage Clerks

Aspect	Detail
Hourly Rate	$28.9
Annual Salary	$60,200
Degree Level Required	High school diploma or equivalent

They work in the financial sector, assisting with the activities related to stocks, bonds, commodities, and other types of investments. They manage and maintain investment portfolios, process transactions, and keep records of financial transactions and securities positions.

Budget Analysts

Aspect	Detail
Hourly Rate	$40.9
Annual Salary	$85,000
Degree Level Required	Bachelor's degree

They help public and private institutions organize their finances. They prepare budget reports and monitor institutional spending with the aim of providing efficient and effective use of funds. Their work involves analyzing data to determine the costs and benefits of various programs and to recommend funding levels based on their findings.

Bus Drivers, School

Aspect	Detail
Hourly Rate	$22
Annual Salary	$45,700
Degree Level Required	High school diploma or equivalent

They are responsible for safely transporting students to and from school and related events. They must follow a set schedule and route, maintain order and safety on the bus, and follow traffic laws and safety regulations. They also need to conduct inspections of the bus before and after each route.

Bus Drivers, Transit and Intercity

Aspect	Detail
Hourly Rate	$24.47
Annual Salary	$50,900
Degree Level Required	High school diploma or equivalent

They drive buses or motor coaches, including charter buses or city buses. They are tasked with following a timetable for a fixed route, collecting fares, and providing information to passengers. They must have a good understanding of their service area to navigate routes effectively and deal with any disruptions or traffic delays.

Business Teachers, Postsecondary

Aspect	Detail
Hourly Rate	$46.7
Annual Salary	$97,200
Degree Level Required	Doctoral or professional degree

They instruct students in a wide array of business disciplines at the college or university level. They prepare and give lectures, grade exams and papers, and conduct research in their field of expertise. Their goal is to educate the next generation of business professionals and scholars.

Butchers and Meat Cutters

Aspect	Detail
Hourly Rate	$18.1
Annual Salary	$37,700
Degree Level Required	No formal educational credential

They process animal carcasses into standard cuts of meat for sale. They operate saws, knives, and specialized equipment to trim, cut, and prepare meat for retail, wholesale, or individual customers. Butchers and meat cutters must adhere to strict food safety and sanitation standards.

Buyers and Purchasing Agents

Aspect	Detail
Hourly Rate	$34.6
Annual Salary	$72,000
Degree Level Required	Bachelor's degree

They source and procure goods and services for organizations. They research suppliers, compare prices and quality, negotiate contracts, and manage inventory levels. Buyers and purchasing agents ensure their organizations have the necessary resources at the best possible prices.

Calibration Technologists and Technicians

Aspect	Detail
Hourly Rate	$30.2
Annual Salary	$62,800
Degree Level Required	Associate's degree

They test, adjust, and calibrate precision measuring instruments used in manufacturing, scientific research, and other technical fields. They ensure the accuracy of critical instruments like gauges, scales, and electronic sensors.

Camera and Photographic Equipment Repairers

Aspect	Detail
Hourly Rate	$22.5
Annual Salary	$46,900
Degree Level Required	High school diploma or equivalent

They repair and maintain cameras and other photographic equipment. They diagnose issues with lenses, shutters, electronics, or film mechanisms. Camera repairers work with both traditional and digital equipment to restore functionality.

Camera Operators, Television, Video, and Film

Aspect	Detail
Hourly Rate	$29.7
Annual Salary	$61,800
Degree Level Required	Bachelor's degree

They control cameras to capture video footage for television shows, movies, news broadcasts, and other productions. They collaborate with directors to frame shots, adjust lighting and settings, and execute complex camera movements according to the director's vision.

Captains, Mates, and Pilots of Water Vessels

Aspect	Detail
Hourly Rate	$42.7
Annual Salary	$88,800
Degree Level Required	Postsecondary non-degree award

They command various watercraft, including ships, ferries, tugboats, and other vessels. Captains have ultimate responsibility for vessel navigation, safety, and cargo or passenger transport. Mates serve as second-in-command, assisting the captain and overseeing the crew. Pilots specialize in navigating challenging waterways such as harbors and rivers.

Cardiologists

Aspect	Detail
Hourly Rate	$132.2
Annual Salary	$275,000
Degree Level Required	Doctoral or professional degree

They are specialized physicians who diagnose and treat diseases of the heart and blood vessels. They perform examinations, interpret diagnostic tests, and manage complex cardiac conditions such as heart attacks, heart rhythm disturbances, and heart failure. Cardiologists often work in hospitals and may perform procedures like cardiac catheterizations or implant pacemakers.

Cardiovascular Technologists and Technicians

Aspect	Detail
Hourly Rate	$31.8
Annual Salary	$66,200
Degree Level Required	Associate's degree

They assist cardiologists in diagnosing and treating cardiac and peripheral vascular ailments. They may specialize in invasive procedures, like catheterizations, non-invasive testing such as echocardiograms, or vascular technology. They prepare patients for procedures, operate equipment, and help analyze findings.

Cargo and Freight Agents

Aspect	Detail
Hourly Rate	$23.3
Annual Salary	$48,400
Degree Level Required	High school diploma or equivalent

They coordinate and facilitate the movement of goods by air, sea, or land. They arrange transportation, track shipments, prepare and process necessary documentation, and ensure compliance with regulations. They also communicate with customers to keep them informed about the status of their shipments.

Carpenters

Aspect	Detail
Hourly Rate	$27.1
Annual Salary	$56,400
Degree Level Required	High school diploma or equivalent

They construct, repair, and install building frameworks and structures made from wood and other materials. This includes constructing building frameworks, including walls, floors, and doorframes, and installing cabinets, siding, and drywall. They interpret blueprints and must be precise with measurements and skilled with a variety of tools.

Carpet Installers

Aspect	Detail
Hourly Rate	$22.9
Annual Salary	$47,600
Degree Level Required	No formal educational credential

They specialize in laying and installing carpet in homes, offices, and other buildings. They must measure the area to be carpeted accurately, prepare the surface, cut the carpet to size, and secure it in place, ensuring a smooth surface without imperfections.

Cartographers and Photogrammetrists

Aspect	Detail
Hourly Rate	$36.7
Annual Salary	$76,300
Degree Level Required	Bachelor's degree

They collect, measure, and interpret geographic information to create and update maps and charts for regional planning, education, emergency response, and other purposes. They use a variety of tools including GIS (Geographic Information Systems) to analyze and visualize data.

Cashiers

Aspect	Detail
Hourly Rate	$14.3
Annual Salary	$29,800
Degree Level Required	No formal educational credential

They handle transactions with customers in retail or other commercial settings. They scan goods, ensure pricing is accurate, collect payments, and issue receipts. Beyond processing transactions, they may also assist in resolving customer issues, maintaining clean and orderly checkout areas, and stocking shelves.

Cement Masons and Concrete Finishers

Aspect	Detail
Hourly Rate	$24.4
Annual Salary	$50,800
Degree Level Required	No formal educational credential

They pour, smooth, and finish concrete for buildings, roads, and other structures. They ensure that the concrete is poured correctly and provide any desired texture to the surface. The work is physically demanding and often done outdoors.

Chefs and Head Cooks

Aspect	Detail
Hourly Rate	$28.4
Annual Salary	$59,000
Degree Level Required	High school diploma or equivalent

They oversee the daily food preparation at restaurants and other places where food is served. They direct kitchen staff, plan menus, ensure food meets quality standards, order supplies, and often develop recipes. They might also be involved in restaurant management, including staff scheduling and budgeting.

Chemical Engineers

Aspect	Detail
Hourly Rate	$53.9
Annual Salary	$112,100
Degree Level Required	Bachelor's degree

They apply the principles of chemistry, physics, math, and engineering to solve problems that involve the production or use of chemicals, fuel, drugs, food, and many other products. They design processes and equipment for large-scale manufacturing, plan and test production methods, and oversee operations.

Chemical Plant and System Operators

Aspect	Detail
Hourly Rate	$38.5
Annual Salary	$80,100
Degree Level Required	High school diploma or equivalent

They control and monitor the machinery and systems used in chemical production processes. They adjust temperatures, pressures, and flow rates, take samples for analysis, and troubleshoot problems to ensure safe and efficient production.

Chief Executives

Aspect	Detail
Hourly Rate	$99.4
Annual Salary	$206,700
Degree Level Required	Bachelor's degree

They hold the highest-ranking position within a company or organization. They set strategic direction, make major corporate decisions, oversee operations, and represent the organization externally.

Childcare Workers

Aspect	Detail
Hourly Rate	$14.6
Annual Salary	$30,400
Degree Level Required	High school diploma or equivalent

They provide care and supervision for infants and young children. They attend to children's basic needs, engage them in activities to promote development, and ensure a safe and nurturing environment. Childcare workers may operate in a variety of settings, from daycare centers to private homes.

Chiropractors

Aspect	Detail
Hourly Rate	$36.8
Annual Salary	$76,600
Degree Level Required	Doctoral or professional degree

They are healthcare professionals who focus on diagnosing and treating disorders of the musculoskeletal system, particularly the spine. They use manual adjustments, spinal manipulation, and other techniques to relieve pain, improve joint function, and support overall health.

Choreographers

Aspect	Detail
Hourly Rate	$25
Annual Salary	$52,000
Degree Level Required	High school diploma or equivalent

They design and create dance sequences for performances. They develop original movements, select music, collaborate with dancers, and oversee rehearsals to bring their artistic vision to life. Choreographers work in a variety of settings, from dance companies to theater productions.

Civil Engineers

Aspect	Detail
Hourly Rate	$46.1
Annual Salary	$95,900
Degree Level Required	Bachelor's degree

They design and oversee the construction of infrastructure projects such as roads, bridges, buildings, dams, and water systems. They conduct site assessments, develop plans, manage budgets, and ensure projects comply with regulations and safety standards.

Claims Adjusters, Examiners, and Investigators

Aspect	Detail
Hourly Rate	$36.1
Annual Salary	$75,100
Degree Level Required	High school diploma or equivalent

They evaluate insurance claims to determine the extent of an insurance company's liability. They investigate claims by gathering evidence, interviewing witnesses, and analyzing policy coverage. Claims professionals determine the validity of claims and the appropriate payout amounts.

Cleaners of Vehicles and Equipment

Aspect	Detail
Hourly Rate	$16.4
Annual Salary	$34,200
Degree Level Required	No formal educational credential

They wash, maintain, and detail the interior and exterior of cars, trucks, construction equipment, and other vehicles. They use a variety of cleaning supplies and tools to remove dirt, stains, and debris.

Cleaning, Washing, and Metal Pickling Equipment Operators

Aspect	Detail
Hourly Rate	$18.9
Annual Salary	$39,400
Degree Level Required	High school diploma or equivalent

They are responsible for operating or tending machines to wash or clean products, such as barrels or kegs, glass items, tin plate, food, pulp, coal, plastic, or rubber, to remove impurities. They set up and control equipment, monitor the cleaning process, and ensure that the items are cleaned to specification.

Clinical and Counseling Psychologists

Aspect	Detail
Hourly Rate	$46.2
Annual Salary	$96,100
Degree Level Required	Doctoral or professional degree

They assess, diagnose, and treat mental, emotional, and behavioral disorders. They provide therapy to individuals and groups, create treatment plans, and might work in various settings, including private practices, hospitals, and schools. They often work collaboratively with other healthcare professionals.

Commercial Divers

Aspect	Detail
Hourly Rate	$29.5
Annual Salary	$61,300
Degree Level Required	Postsecondary non-degree award

They work underwater to repair, install, or remove equipment and structures. They may conduct tests or experiments, rig explosives, or photograph structures or marine life. Diving for commercial purposes requires strict adherence to safety and health regulations.

Commercial Pilots

Aspect	Detail
Hourly Rate	$54.4
Annual Salary	$113,100
Degree Level Required	Postsecondary non-degree award

They fly aircraft for purposes other than military or scheduled airline flights, which may include charter flights, rescue operations, firefighting, and aerial photography. They must check the condition of the aircraft before and after flights and operate the aircraft safely and efficiently.

Communications Teachers, Postsecondary

Aspect	Detail
Hourly Rate	$38.5
Annual Salary	$80,000
Degree Level Required	Doctoral or professional degree

They educate students in subjects such as communication theory, media studies, rhetoric, and public relations. They prepare and deliver lectures, grade papers, conduct research, and may work on committees to improve educational institutions.

Compensation and Benefits Managers

Aspect	Detail
Hourly Rate	$65.6
Annual Salary	$136,400
Degree Level Required	Bachelor's degree

They oversee an organization's compensation and benefits programs, including salaries, retirement plans, health insurance, and other employee perks. They ensure that these programs are competitive, sustainable, and comply with legal requirements.

Compliance Officers

Aspect	Detail
Hourly Rate	$36.4
Annual Salary	$75,700
Degree Level Required	Bachelor's degree

They ensure that organizations adhere to laws and regulations applicable to their industry. They conduct audits, investigate compliance issues, and work with management to address any violations and prevent future breaches.

Computer and Information Research Scientists

Aspect	Detail
Hourly Rate	$69 8
Annual Salary	$145,100
Degree Level Required	Master's degree

They invent and design new approaches to computing technology and find innovative uses for existing technology. They study complex problems in computing for business, science, medicine, and other fields.

Computer and Information Systems Managers

Aspect	Detail
Hourly Rate	$81.5
Annual Salary	$169,600
Degree Level Required	Bachelor's degree

They plan, coordinate, and direct computer-related activities in an organization. They help determine the information technology goals of an organization and are responsible for implementing computer systems to meet those goals.

Computer Hardware Engineers

Aspect	Detail
Hourly Rate	$66.4
Annual Salary	$138,100
Degree Level Required	Bachelor's degree

They research, design, develop, and test computer systems and components such as processors, circuit boards, memory devices, networks, and routers. They ensure that hardware works correctly with the latest software developments.

Computer Programmers

Aspect	Detail
Hourly Rate	$47.9
Annual Salary	$99,700
Degree Level Required	Bachelor's degree

They write and test code that allows computer applications and software programs to function properly. They turn the program designs created by software developers and engineers into instructions that a computer can follow.

Computer Science Teachers, Postsecondary

Aspect	Detail
Hourly Rate	$46.4
Annual Salary	$96,500
Degree Level Required	Doctoral or professional degree

They teach courses in computer science to college or university students. They prepare lectures, assignments, and exams, conduct research, publish scholarly papers, and stay updated on technological advances in the field.

Computer Systems Analysts

Aspect	Detail
Hourly Rate	$49.9
Annual Salary	$103,800
Degree Level Required	Bachelor's degree

They study organizations' computer systems and procedures to recommend solutions that increase efficiency and effectiveness. They analyze needs, design new systems, implement upgrades, and may train staff on the new technologies.

Computer User Support Specialists

Aspect	Detail
Hourly Rate	$28.5
Annual Salary	$59,300
Degree Level Required	Some college, no degree

They also known as help desk technicians, assist people experiencing computer problems. They troubleshoot software and hardware issues, provide advice, and help users understand their computer systems.

Concierges

Aspect	Detail
Hourly Rate	$17.9
Annual Salary	$37,200
Degree Level Required	High school diploma or equivalent

They often found at hotels and resorts, provide guests with personalized services to enhance their stay. They make reservations, secure tickets to shows and events, arrange transportation, offer recommendations, and handle special requests.

Conservation Scientists

Aspect	Detail
Hourly Rate	$33.1
Annual Salary	$68,800
Degree Level Required	Bachelor's degree

They manage, improve, and protect natural resources. They research land-use practices, analyze environmental problems, develop conservation plans, and may work to restore degraded habitats.

Construction and Building Inspectors

Aspect	Detail
Hourly Rate	$32.5
Annual Salary	$67,700
Degree Level Required	High school diploma or equivalent

They examine buildings and construction sites to ensure compliance with building codes, regulations, and safety standards. They inspect structural elements, electrical systems, plumbing, and other aspects of construction.

Construction Laborers

Aspect	Detail
Hourly Rate	$21.8
Annual Salary	$45,300
Degree Level Required	No formal educational credential

They perform various physically demanding tasks on construction sites. They assist skilled tradespeople, demolish structures, operate hand and power tools, move materials, and clean up debris.

Construction Managers

Aspect	Detail
Hourly Rate	$50.4
Annual Salary	$104,900
Degree Level Required	Bachelor's degree

They plan, coordinate, and oversee construction projects. They manage budgets, schedules, contracts, and workers to ensure projects are completed on time, within budget, and to a high quality standard.

Cooks, Fast Food

Aspect	Detail
Hourly Rate	$14.1
Annual Salary	$29,300
Degree Level Required	No formal educational credential

They prepare and cook food items in quick-service restaurants. They follow standardized recipes, operate kitchen equipment, and assemble orders quickly and accurately.

Cooks, Private Household

Aspect	Detail
Hourly Rate	$20.5
Annual Salary	$42,600
Degree Level Required	Postsecondary non-degree award

They prepare meals for families or individuals in a home setting. They may follow recipes developed by their employers, create menus, shop for groceries, and serve meals.

Cooks, Restaurant

Aspect	Detail
Hourly Rate	$17.2
Annual Salary	$35,800
Degree Level Required	No formal educational credential

They manage, improve, and protect natural resources. They research land-use practices, analyze environmental problems, develop conservation plans, and may work to restore degraded habitats.

Correctional Officers and Jailers

Aspect	Detail
Hourly Rate	$25.6
Annual Salary	$53,300
Degree Level Required	High school diploma or equivalent

They are responsible for overseeing individuals who have been arrested and are awaiting trial or who have been sentenced to serve time in a jail or prison. Their duties include maintaining security and order within the institution, supervising the activities of inmates, inspecting facilities for contraband, and enforcing rules and regulations.

Correspondence Clerks

Aspect	Detail
Hourly Rate	$20.3
Annual Salary	$42,200
Degree Level Required	High school diploma or equivalent

They manage communication in various forms, including letters, emails, and other documents. They ensure that information is disseminated appropriately, responses are drafted and sent in a timely manner, and that all correspondences are logged and archived according to company policy.

Cost Estimators

Aspect	Detail
Hourly Rate	$36
Annual Salary	$74,800
Degree Level Required	Bachelor's degree

They calculate the time, money, materials, and labor required to manufacture a product, construct a building, or provide a service. They often specialize in a particular product or industry and use software to analyze data and provide accurate estimates to inform financial decisions.

Couriers and Messengers

Aspect	Detail
Hourly Rate	$17.7
Annual Salary	$36,800
Degree Level Required	High school diploma or equivalent

They provide and transport documents and physical items, often within a local area. They ensure the secure and timely delivery of parcels, documents, and other items, and may require knowledge of delivery routes and customer service skills.

Court Reporters and Simultaneous Captioners

Aspect	Detail
Hourly Rate	$30.8
Annual Salary	$64,000
Degree Level Required	Postsecondary non-degree award

They create word-for-word transcriptions at trials, depositions, administrative hearings, and may provide captioning for television and real-time translation for deaf or hard-of-hearing people at public events, in business meetings, or in classrooms.

Court, Municipal, and License Clerks

Aspect	Detail
Hourly Rate	$22.2
Annual Salary	$46,200
Degree Level Required	High school diploma or equivalent

They perform clerical duties in courts of law, municipalities, and governmental licensing agencies and bureaus. They assist in the administration of government functions, and may serve the public by filing and retrieving documents, processing licenses, and providing information.

Craft Artists

Aspect	Detail
Hourly Rate	$17.6
Annual Salary	$36,600
Degree Level Required	No formal educational credential

They create artwork by hand, using a variety of materials and techniques. They sell their works to the public, often at craft fairs, shops, and galleries, and may also conduct workshops or demonstrations to share their skills.

Crane and Tower Operators

Aspect	Detail
Hourly Rate	$31.1
Annual Salary	$64,700
Degree Level Required	High school diploma or equivalent

They control mechanical boom and cable or tower and cable equipment to lift and move materials, machines, or products in many directions. They are critical in construction sites and other industrial settings, following safety standards strictly.

Credit Analysts

Aspect	Detail
Hourly Rate	$38.2
Annual Salary	$79,500
Degree Level Required	Bachelor's degree

They assess the creditworthiness of individuals or businesses and advise banks, credit card companies, or other financial institutions about the risks involved in lending money or extending credit. They analyze financial data and create reports for use in decision-making.

Crematory Operators

Aspect	Detail
Hourly Rate	$20
Annual Salary	$41,700
Degree Level Required	High school diploma or equivalent

They perform cremations and maintain cremation equipment. They handle the administrative and technical tasks involved in cremating human remains, ensuring respectful handling and compliance with all relevant laws and regulations.

Curators

Aspect	Detail
Hourly Rate	$29.7
Annual Salary	$61,800
Degree Level Required	Master's degree

They oversee collections of artwork and historic items and may conduct public service activities for an institution. They manage the acquisition, storage, and exhibition of collections, including negotiating the loan of artwork and arranging for its transport.

Customer Service Representatives

Aspect	Detail
Hourly Rate	$19.1
Annual Salary	$39,700
Degree Level Required	High school diploma or equivalent

They interact with customers to handle complaints, process orders, and provide information about an organization's products and services. They may communicate with customers by telephone, email, chat, or in person.

Dancers

Aspect	Detail
Hourly Rate	$24.95
Annual Salary	$51,900
Degree Level Required	No formal educational credential

They use movement to express ideas and stories in performances. They may perform in a variety of settings, from theaters and dance companies to films, TV, and music videos. They typically audition for roles and spend long hours rehearsing.

Data Entry Keyers

Aspect	Detail
Hourly Rate	$18.2
Annual Salary	$37,800
Degree Level Required	High school diploma or equivalent

They input information into computer systems from various sources like handwritten forms, documents, or audio files. They focus on speed and accuracy while entering data into databases or spreadsheets.

Data Scientists

Aspect	Detail
Hourly Rate	$52
Annual Salary	$108,100
Degree Level Required	Bachelor's degree

They collect, clean, analyze, and interpret large, complex datasets. They use statistical techniques, programming skills, and machine learning to uncover patterns, trends, and insights from data, helping organizations make informed decisions.

Database Administrators

Aspect	Detail
Hourly Rate	$48.8
Annual Salary	$101,600
Degree Level Required	Bachelor's degree

They install, configure, manage, and maintain the databases that store an organization's critical information. They ensure database security, optimize performance, troubleshoot issues, and back up data to prevent loss.

Database Architects

Aspect	Detail
Hourly Rate	$64.8
Annual Salary	$134,700
Degree Level Required	Bachelor's degree

They design the structure and organization of large-scale databases. They determine the most appropriate data models, storage technologies, and access methods to align with an organization's specific needs.

Dental Assistants

Aspect	Detail
Hourly Rate	$22.4
Annual Salary	$46,600
Degree Level Required	Postsecondary non-degree award

They work alongside dentists to provide patient care. They prepare patients for treatment, take x-rays, sterilize instruments, assist during procedures, and educate patients on oral healthcare.

Dental Hygienists

Aspect	Detail
Hourly Rate	$42.1
Annual Salary	$87,600
Degree Level Required	Associate's degree

They clean teeth, examine patients for signs of oral disease, provide preventive dental care, and educate patients on good oral hygiene practices.

Dentists, General

Aspect	Detail
Hourly Rate	$80
Annual Salary	$166,300
Degree Level Required	Doctoral or professional degree

They are primary dental care providers. They diagnose and treat a wide range of oral health issues including cavities, gum disease, and tooth pain. They may also perform fillings, extractions, root canals, and other dental procedures.

Dermatologists

Aspect	Detail
Hourly Rate	$127.40
Annual Salary	$265,000
Degree Level Required	Doctoral or professional degree

They are doctors specializing in diagnosing and treating disorders of the skin, hair, and nails. They treat conditions such as acne, eczema, psoriasis, skin cancer, and address cosmetic concerns related to skin.

Derrick Operators, Oil and Gas

Aspect	Detail
Hourly Rate	$28
Annual Salary	$58,300
Degree Level Required	No formal educational credential

They handle the equipment used to extract oil and gas from underground wells. They oversee the derricks on drilling rigs and work with teams to guide the drilling equipment in and out of drill holes. Safety is a paramount concern, as they must handle complex machinery and sometimes work in hazardous conditions.

Detectives and Criminal Investigators

Aspect	Detail
Hourly Rate	$43.8
Annual Salary	$91,100
Degree Level Required	High school diploma or equivalent

They gather facts and collect evidence for criminal cases. They conduct interviews, examine records, observe the activities of suspects, and participate in raids or arrests. Detectives typically specialize in investigating a range of criminal activities such as homicide, cybercrime, or fraud.

Diagnostic Medical Sonographers

Aspect	Detail
Hourly Rate	$40.6
Annual Salary	$84,500
Degree Level Required	Associate's degree

They specialize in using ultrasonic imaging devices to produce diagnostic images, scans, videos, or 3D volumes of anatomy and diagnostic data. They work with physicians to detect, diagnose, and treat various medical conditions and must be skilled at patient interaction and operating ultrasound equipment.

Dietitians and Nutritionists

Aspect	Detail
Hourly Rate	$33.5
Annual Salary	$69,700
Degree Level Required	Bachelor's degree

They provide expert advice on proper eating habits to help promote overall health and manage diseases. They assess patients' nutritional needs, develop meal plans, evaluate the effects of the plan, and change it as needed. They work in various settings, including hospitals, clinics, and public health agencies.

Dining Room and Cafeteria Attendants and Bartender Helpers

Aspect	Detail
Hourly Rate	$15
Annual Salary	$31,200
Degree Level Required	No formal educational credential

They work in the hospitality industry, assisting in dining environments. They help waitstaff by setting and clearing tables, keeping dining areas clean, and assisting bartenders with stocking and cleaning.

Dishwashers

Aspect	Detail
Hourly Rate	$15
Annual Salary	$31,200
Degree Level Required	No formal educational credential

They are responsible for maintaining cleanliness and hygiene in the kitchen, washing dishes, glassware, flatware, pots, or pans, using dishwashers or by hand, and sometimes helping with food preparation.

Driver/Sales Workers

Aspect	Detail
Hourly Rate	$17.1
Annual Salary	$35,500
Degree Level Required	High school diploma or equivalent

They operate vehicles to deliver goods to customers, and they also manage sales transactions for the delivery of these goods. They are responsible for inventory, sales records, and customer service during deliveries.

Drywall and Ceiling Tile Installers

Aspect	Detail
Hourly Rate	$26.8
Annual Salary	$55,700
Degree Level Required	No formal educational credential

They hang wallboard and install ceiling tile inside buildings. They use trowels, brushes, and texturing tools to finish and repair walls in preparation for painting or wallpapering.

Earth Drillers, Except Oil and Gas

Aspect	Detail
Hourly Rate	$27.3
Annual Salary	$56,700
Degree Level Required	High school diploma or equivalent

They operate a variety of drills to remove underground oil and gas, or to remove core samples for testing during mineral exploration or soil testing. They are skilled in operating drilling machinery and often work in resource extraction or construction.

Economics Teachers, Postsecondary

Aspect	Detail
Hourly Rate	$55.4
Annual Salary	$115,300
Degree Level Required	Doctoral or professional degree

They instruct students in economics at colleges and universities. They teach a range of economic subjects, advise students, and conduct research. They often publish their findings in books or scholarly articles.

Economists

Aspect	Detail
Hourly Rate	$55.7
Annual Salary	$115,800
Degree Level Required	Master's degree

They study how society distributes resources, such as land, labor, raw materials, and machinery, to produce goods and services. They conduct research, collect and analyze data, monitor economic trends, and develop forecasts.

Editors

Aspect	Detail
Hourly Rate	$36.1
Annual Salary	$75,100
Degree Level Required	Bachelor's degree

They plan, coordinate, and revise material for publication in books, newspapers, magazines, or websites. They review story ideas, decide what material will appeal to readers, and oversee the production of publications. They may also suggest revisions to authors and ensure that materials adhere to established styles and themes.

Education Administrators, Kindergarten through Secondary

Aspect	Detail
Hourly Rate	$49.8
Annual Salary	$103,500
Degree Level Required	Master's degree

They are professionals who manage the day-to-day operations of K-12 schools. They set educational goals and standards, establish policies and procedures, oversee staff, manage budgets, and interact with students and parents. Their leadership helps shape the educational experience and environment.

Electric Motor, Power Tool, and Related Repairers

Aspect	Detail
Hourly Rate	$23.7
Annual Salary	$49,300
Degree Level Required	High school diploma or equivalent

They specialize in the maintenance and repair of electrical motors, power tools, and other related equipment. They troubleshoot issues, replace parts, and ensure that machinery operates efficiently and safely.

Electrical and Electronics Installers and Repairers

Aspect	Detail
Hourly Rate	$38.1
Annual Salary	$79,200
Degree Level Required	Postsecondary non-degree award

They focus on the installation, testing, maintenance, and repair of a variety of electrical equipment for commercial, industrial, and transportation sectors. This includes ensuring that electrical systems work correctly and meet safety standards.

Electrical Engineers

Aspect	Detail
Hourly Rate	$51.4
Annual Salary	$107,000
Degree Level Required	Bachelor's degree

They design, develop, test, and supervise the manufacturing of electrical equipment, such as electric motors, radar and navigation systems, communications systems, or power generation equipment. They also work on a variety of projects from small-scale electronics to large power networks.

Electrical Power-Line Installers and Repairers

Aspect	Detail
Hourly Rate	$41.1
Annual Salary	$85,500
Degree Level Required	High school diploma or equivalent

They are responsible for installing, maintaining, and repairing the power grid. They work on the various components required to transmit electricity from power plants to consumers, often at great heights and under challenging conditions.

Electricians

Aspect	Detail
Hourly Rate	$29.6
Annual Salary	$61,600
Degree Level Required	High school diploma or equivalent

They install, maintain, and repair electrical wiring, equipment, and fixtures. They ensure that work is in accordance with relevant codes and may install or service street lights, intercom systems, or electrical control systems.

Electronics Engineers, Except Computer

Aspect	Detail
Hourly Rate	$57.3
Annual Salary	$119,200
Degree Level Required	Bachelor's degree

They work on designing and developing electronic components like broadcast and communications systems, from portable music players to global positioning systems (GPS). These engineers apply principles and theories of electronics to create and improve devices and systems.

Elementary School Teachers, Except Special Education

Aspect	Detail
Hourly Rate	$30.6
Annual Salary	$63,700
Degree Level Required	Bachelor's degree

They instruct young students in basic subjects such as math and reading. They prepare lesson plans, evaluate student performance, and aim to build a strong educational foundation for each child.

Elevator and Escalator Installers and Repairers

Aspect	Detail
Hourly Rate	$49.3
Annual Salary	$102,500
Degree Level Required	High school diploma or equivalent

They specialize in the installation, maintenance, and repair of elevators, escalators, moving walkways, and other lifts. Their work requires knowledge of electronics, hydraulics, and electricity.

Embalmers

Aspect	Detail
Hourly Rate	$26
Annual Salary	$54,100
Degree Level Required	Associate's degree

They are professionals in the funeral service industry who prepare bodies for burial or cremation. They sanitize, preserve, and restore the appearance of the deceased, often working with funeral directors to ensure that loved ones' preferences are met.

Emergency Management Directors

Aspect	Detail
Hourly Rate	$40.4
Annual Salary	$84,000
Degree Level Required	Bachelor's degree

They develop and implement plans to prepare for and respond to natural disasters, technological accidents, or other major emergencies. They coordinate with various agencies, manage resources, and oversee training and public outreach efforts to ensure community safety.

Emergency Medicine Physicians

Aspect	Detail
Hourly Rate	$122.6
Annual Salary	$255,000
Degree Level Required	Doctoral or professional degree

They work in hospital emergency departments, providing immediate care to patients with acute illnesses and injuries. They rapidly assess, diagnose, and treat a broad range of life-threatening conditions.

Engine and Other Machine Assemblers

Aspect	Detail
Hourly Rate	$24.2
Annual Salary	$50,300
Degree Level Required	High school diploma or equivalent

They build and assemble engines, turbines, and various other types of machinery according to blueprints and specifications. They use hand and power tools to fit, align, and connect the components of complex machinery.

Environmental Engineers

Aspect	Detail
Hourly Rate	$48.1
Annual Salary	$100,100
Degree Level Required	Bachelor's degree

They use the principles of engineering to address environmental problems. They design systems for pollution control, water treatment, waste management, and sustainable resource use. Environmental engineers work to protect public health and the environment.

Epidemiologists

Aspect	Detail
Hourly Rate	$39.1
Annual Salary	$81,400
Degree Level Required	Master's degree

They investigate patterns and causes of diseases within populations. They collect and analyze data, design studies, identify risk factors, and develop strategies to prevent and control outbreaks of disease.

Etchers and Engravers

Aspect	Detail
Hourly Rate	$19.3
Annual Salary	$40,100
Degree Level Required	High school diploma or equivalent

They mark designs onto metal, glass, or other materials using hand tools, chemicals, or by directing laser beams. They create decorative designs, patterns, or print inscriptions.

Excavating and Loading Operators, Surface Mining

Aspect	Detail
Hourly Rate	$24.1
Annual Salary	$50,100
Degree Level Required	High school diploma or equivalent

They run large machinery to excavate and load earth, rock, or other materials in surface mines and quarries. They operate bulldozers, draglines, power shovels, and other heavy equipment to remove and transport resources.

Executive Secretaries and Executive Administrative Assistants

Aspect	Detail
Hourly Rate	$33.8
Annual Salary	$70,400
Degree Level Required	High school diploma or equivalent

They provide high-level support to executives in organizations. They manage schedules, organize travel, prepare correspondence, handle complex office tasks, and often serve as the first point of contact for important communications.

Exercise Physiologists

Aspect	Detail
Hourly Rate	$26.4
Annual Salary	$54,900
Degree Level Required	Bachelor's degree

They develop fitness and exercise programs tailored to improve health, manage chronic conditions, or enhance sports performance. They assess fitness levels, design safe and effective exercise plans, and monitor progress.

Exercise Trainers and Group Fitness Instructors

Aspect	Detail
Hourly Rate	$22.4
Annual Salary	$46,500
Degree Level Required	High school diploma or equivalent

They lead individuals and groups through exercise routines. They demonstrate exercises, provide guidance on proper form, may modify exercises for different fitness levels, and motivate participants.

Explosives Workers, Ordnance Handling Experts, and Blasters

Aspect	Detail
Hourly Rate	$29.6
Annual Salary	$61,600
Degree Level Required	High school diploma or equivalent

They handle and detonate explosives for various purposes. They may work in mining, demolition, construction, or military settings. They follow strict safety protocols to transport, prepare, and detonate explosives under controlled conditions.

Extruding, Forming, Pressing, and Compacting Operators

Aspect	Detail
Hourly Rate	$20.5
Annual Salary	$42,700
Degree Level Required	High school diploma or equivalent

They operate machinery that shapes and forms various materials. They are responsible for setting up the machines, ensuring materials are fed into the machines correctly, and monitoring the machinery for quality and efficiency during operation.

Fabric and Apparel Patternmakers

Aspect	Detail
Hourly Rate	$30.1
Annual Salary	$62,600
Degree Level Required	High school diploma or equivalent

They create patterns for garments. They use design sketches and specifications to draft the outlines of pieces of a garment onto paper or computer, which are then used to cut the fabric into the correct shapes before being sewn into finished clothing.

Facilities Managers

Aspect	Detail
Hourly Rate	$49.2
Annual Salary	$102,400
Degree Level Required	Bachelor's degree

They oversee the maintenance, operation, and planning of buildings and grounds. They ensure that the facilities meet government regulations and environmental, health, and security standards. They coordinate renovations, manage budgets, and supervise maintenance and custodial staff.

Fallers

Aspect	Detail
Hourly Rate	$25.6
Annual Salary	$53,200
Degree Level Required	High school diploma or equivalent

They are skilled workers who cut down trees using axes or chainsaws. They work in the logging industry and must have a strong understanding of tree characteristics and cutting techniques to control the direction of a tree's fall safely.

Family Medicine Physicians

Aspect	Detail
Hourly Rate	$108
Annual Salary	$224,700
Degree Level Required	Doctoral or professional degree

They provide comprehensive health care for individuals and families across all ages, genders, diseases, and parts of the body. They are often primary care providers and are trained to treat a wide range of health issues.

Farm Equipment Mechanics and Service Technicians

Aspect	Detail
Hourly Rate	$23.7
Annual Salary	$49,300
Degree Level Required	High school diploma or equivalent

They repair and maintain the machinery used in agriculture, such as tractors and harvesters. They work to keep farm operations running smoothly, often troubleshooting and repairing complex mechanical, hydraulic, and electrical systems.

Fashion Designers

Aspect	Detail
Hourly Rate	$38.1
Annual Salary	$79,300
Degree Level Required	Bachelor's degree

They create original clothing, accessories, and footwear. They sketch designs, select fabrics and patterns, and give instructions on how to make the products they have designed. They must stay current with trends and consumer preferences.

Fast Food and Counter Workers

Aspect	Detail
Hourly Rate	$14.2
Annual Salary	$29,600
Degree Level Required	No formal educational credential

They serve customers in fast-food restaurants. Their tasks include taking orders, preparing food, ensuring cleanliness, and handling cash. They must work quickly and efficiently to meet the high-paced demand of the environment.

Fence Erectors

Aspect	Detail
Hourly Rate	$21.4
Annual Salary	$44,500
Degree Level Required	No formal educational credential

They install and repair fences and gates. They work with a variety of materials, including wood, metal, and vinyl, to create barriers that provide privacy, security, or decoration for residential or commercial properties.

Fiberglass Laminators and Fabricators

Aspect	Detail
Hourly Rate	$19.3
Annual Salary	$40,200
Degree Level Required	High school diploma or equivalent

They manipulate fiberglass materials to create products. They must follow strict safety guidelines while cutting, shaping, and bonding materials to form parts for various industries, such as automotive or marine.

Film and Video Editors

Aspect	Detail
Hourly Rate	$32
Annual Salary	$66,600
Degree Level Required	Bachelor's degree

They work with producers and directors to edit moving images on film, video, or other media. They select shots, combine footage, and work with light, sound, and graphics to create a final product that tells a cohesive story.

Financial and Investment Analysts

Aspect	Detail
Hourly Rate	$47.6
Annual Salary	$99,100
Degree Level Required	Bachelor's degree

They examine financial data and trends to provide guidance to businesses and individuals making investment decisions. They assess the performance of stocks, bonds, and other types of investments.

Financial Managers

Aspect	Detail
Hourly Rate	$75
Annual Salary	$156,100
Degree Level Required	Bachelor's degree

They are responsible for the financial health of an organization. They produce financial reports, direct investment activities, and develop strategies and plans for the long-term financial goals of their organization.

Financial Risk Specialists

Aspect	Detail
Hourly Rate	$51
Annual Salary	$106,100
Degree Level Required	Bachelor's degree

They analyze potential risks that could affect the financial profile of organizations. They use their expertise to identify, evaluate, and prioritize risks, which may include market risk, credit risk, or operational risk, and recommend strategies to mitigate or manage these risks.

Fine Artists, Including Painters, Sculptors, and Illustrators

Aspect	Detail
Hourly Rate	$28.5
Annual Salary	$59,300
Degree Level Required	Bachelor's degree

They create original artwork using a variety of media and techniques. Fine artists may sell their work to collectors, museums, or galleries, take on commissions, or display their work in studios and exhibitions.

Fire Inspectors and Investigators

Aspect	Detail
Hourly Rate	$35.7
Annual Salary	$74,200
Degree Level Required	Postsecondary non-degree award

They examine buildings to detect fire hazards and ensure that federal, state, and local fire codes are met. They also investigate the cause of fires and explosions, often working closely with police departments to collect evidence if the fire is suspected to be arson.

Firefighters

Aspect	Detail
Hourly Rate	$27.5
Annual Salary	$57,200
Degree Level Required	Postsecondary non-degree award

They are responsible for extinguishing fires, protecting life and property, and conducting rescue efforts. They often handle emergency medical situations and may conduct fire safety inspections and public education programs on fire prevention.

Flight Attendants

Aspect	Detail
Hourly Rate	$32.9
Annual Salary	$68,400
Degree Level Required	High school diploma or equivalent

They ensure the safety and comfort of passengers aboard flights. Their duties include demonstrating emergency procedures, serving food and drinks, and attending to passengers' needs. They are trained to handle emergencies and enforce regulations during flights.

Floor Sanders and Finishers

Aspect	Detail
Hourly Rate	$23
Annual Salary	$47,800
Degree Level Required	No formal educational credential

They sand and finish wooden floors. They use a variety of sanding machines and coating materials to create smooth, finished surfaces on new floors and to refinish existing floors.

Floral Designers

Aspect	Detail
Hourly Rate	$16.7
Annual Salary	$34,700
Degree Level Required	High school diploma or equivalent

They create decorative displays of flowers. They design bouquets, wreaths, and arrangements for various occasions, using their creativity to combine flowers, greenery, and other items.

Food and Tobacco Roasting, Baking, and Drying Machine Operators

Aspect	Detail
Hourly Rate	$19.2
Annual Salary	$39,900
Degree Level Required	No formal educational credential

They operate machines that roast, bake, or dry food or tobacco products. They set up, tend, operate, and maintain the machinery that processes these products.

Food Batchmakers

Aspect	Detail
Hourly Rate	$18.5
Annual Salary	$38,500
Degree Level Required	High school diploma or equivalent

They follow recipes to make large quantities of food, candies, or baked goods. They operate equipment that mixes, blends, cooks, or processes ingredients in the manufacturing of food products.

Food Cooking Machine Operators and Tenders

Aspect	Detail
Hourly Rate	$18.6
Annual Salary	$38,600
Degree Level Required	High school diploma or equivalent

They operate and maintain equipment that cooks food products. They may set temperatures, monitor cooking times, and check product quality as part of their routine tasks.

Food Scientists and Technologists

Aspect	Detail
Hourly Rate	$39.5
Annual Salary	$82,100
Degree Level Required	Bachelor's degree

They work to improve food products and create new ones using scientific principles. They study the content of food, research ways to make processed foods safe and healthy, and discover new food sources. They work to ensure that food production methods are efficient, sustainable, and meet government regulations.

Foreign Language and Literature Teachers, Postsecondary

Aspect	Detail
Hourly Rate	$37.9
Annual Salary	$78,800
Degree Level Required	Doctoral or professional degree

They teach courses in foreign languages and literature at colleges and universities. They instruct students on grammar, vocabulary, pronunciation, and cultural aspects of the language. They may also teach literature courses, analyzing texts and exploring themes within the context of the language.

Forensic Science Technicians

Aspect	Detail
Hourly Rate	$31.3
Annual Salary	$65,000
Degree Level Required	Bachelor's degree

They assist in criminal investigations by collecting, processing and analyzing evidence at crime scenes and in laboratories. They use scientific techniques to examine fingerprints, DNA, trace materials, and other evidence to support criminal investigations.

Forest and Conservation Technicians

Aspect	Detail
Hourly Rate	$25
Annual Salary	$51,900
Degree Level Required	Associate's degree

They work to protect, manage, and restore forests and wildlands. They may collect data on tree species and forest health, assist with wildfire suppression, implement conservation plans, or monitor habitats.

Foresters

Aspect	Detail
Hourly Rate	$32.4
Annual Salary	$67,400
Degree Level Required	Bachelor's degree

They manage and oversee the sustainable use of forests. They develop forest management plans, assess timber resources, protect forests from pests and diseases, and may oversee forestry operations like tree planting and harvesting.

Forging Machine Setters, Operators, and Tenders, Metal and Plastic

Aspect	Detail
Hourly Rate	$22.6
Annual Salary	$47,000
Degree Level Required	High school diploma or equivalent

They set up, operate, or maintain forging machines that shape metal or plastic by applying heat and high pressure. They adjust machine settings, monitor the forging process, and ensure the quality of the forged products.

Foundry Mold and Coremakers

Aspect	Detail
Hourly Rate	$21.3
Annual Salary	$44,300
Degree Level Required	High school diploma or equivalent

They create the molds and sand cores used in metal casting. They shape sand into molds and cores using patterns and specialized tools, ensuring these forms will create the desired shape when molten metal is poured in.

Fundraising Managers

Aspect	Detail
Hourly Rate	$57.3
Annual Salary	$119,200
Degree Level Required	Bachelor's degree

They oversee the fundraising efforts of non-profit organizations. They develop fundraising strategies, plan campaigns, cultivate relationships with donors, and manage grants or other fundraising initiatives.

Funeral Home Managers

Aspect	Detail
Hourly Rate	$36.4
Annual Salary	$75,700
Degree Level Required	Associate's degree

They oversee the operations of funeral homes. They work with families of the deceased to plan funeral arrangements, manage administrative tasks, ensure compliance with regulations, and supervise funeral home staff.

Furniture Finishers

Aspect	Detail
Hourly Rate	$19.1
Annual Salary	$39,800
Degree Level Required	High school diploma or equivalent

They apply stains, varnishes, or other finishes to wooden furniture to enhance its appearance and protect it from wear. They sand, prepare surfaces, apply finishes using various techniques, and may also repair damaged finishes.

Gambling and Sports Book Writers and Runners

Aspect	Detail
Hourly Rate	$14
Annual Salary	$29,200
Degree Level Required	High school diploma or equivalent

They assist in the operations of games such as keno and bingo. They write tickets for customers, calculate and distribute winnings, and run bets to bookmakers. Their role is crucial in ensuring that gambling operations run smoothly and efficiently.

Gambling Dealers

Aspect	Detail
Hourly Rate	$15.5
Annual Salary	$32,300
Degree Level Required	High school diploma or equivalent

They operate table games such as craps, blackjack, and roulette. They are responsible for dealing cards, spinning wheels, announcing winning numbers or combinations, and ensuring that the rules of the games are followed by players. Dealers also manage the chips and pay out winnings.

Gambling Surveillance Officers and Gambling Investigators

Aspect	Detail
Hourly Rate	$18.90
Annual Salary	$39,300
Degree Level Required	High school diploma or equivalent

They are tasked with overseeing casino operations to prevent cheating, theft, and other illegal or unauthorized activities. They use audio and video technology to monitor behavior and ensure compliance with laws and regulations. Investigators may also conduct investigations into suspicious activities.

Gas Compressor and Gas Pumping Station Operators

Aspect	Detail
Hourly Rate	$29.8
Annual Salary	$61,900
Degree Level Required	High school diploma or equivalent

They manage the operation of engines and equipment to move gas through pipelines or to compress natural gas. They monitor equipment, maintain pressure levels, and ensure the safe and efficient operation of the gas transmission systems.

Gas Plant Operators

Aspect	Detail
Hourly Rate	$39.7
Annual Salary	$82,600
Degree Level Required	High school diploma or equivalent

They control the processing of natural gas. They oversee the operation of equipment that processes gas for utility companies and monitor systems to ensure that products meet quality specifications. Their responsibilities include adjusting controls, performing maintenance, and ensuring safety protocols are followed.

General Internal Medicine Physicians

Aspect	Detail
Hourly Rate	$107.4
Annual Salary	$223,400
Degree Level Required	Doctoral or professional degree

They specialize in diagnosing and providing non-surgical treatment for a wide range of diseases and injuries of the internal organ systems. They provide care mainly for adults and may handle complex illnesses involving multiple systems or chronic conditions.

Genetic Counselors

Aspect	Detail
Hourly Rate	$46.1
Annual Salary	$95,800
Degree Level Required	Master's degree

They assess individual or family risk for a variety of inherited conditions, such as genetic disorders and birth defects. They provide information and advice to patients or families about genetic risks, testing, and potential treatments or interventions.

Geographers

Aspect	Detail
Hourly Rate	$43.7
Annual Salary	$90,900
Degree Level Required	Bachelor's degree

They study the Earth's surface, landscapes, environments, and the relationships between people and their environments. They may specialize in physical geography, human geography, or Geographic Information Systems (GIS) and use various methods to collect, analyze, and interpret geographic information.

Geoscientists, Except Hydrologists and Geographers

Aspect	Detail
Hourly Rate	$44.5
Annual Salary	$92,600
Degree Level Required	Bachelor's degree

They explore the composition, structure, and other physical aspects of the Earth. They may study natural resources, help to plan new developments, or work on environmental protection. Their work often involves field studies and laboratory analysis.

Graphic Designers

Aspect	Detail
Hourly Rate	$28.4
Annual Salary	$59,000
Degree Level Required	Bachelor's degree

They create visual concepts, using computer software or by hand, to communicate ideas that inspire, inform, or captivate consumers. They develop the overall layout and production design for applications such as advertisements, brochures, magazines, and corporate reports.

Hairdressers, Hairstylists, and Cosmetologists

Aspect	Detail
Hourly Rate	$16.8
Annual Salary	$35,000
Degree Level Required	Postsecondary non-degree award

They offer a range of beauty services, such as shampooing, cutting, coloring, and styling hair. They may also provide scalp treatments and facial hair maintenance and may offer advice on how to maintain hairstyles at home.

Hazardous Materials Removal Workers

Aspect	Detail
Hourly Rate	$22.7
Annual Salary	$47,300
Degree Level Required	High school diploma or equivalent

They specialize in the cleanup and disposal of hazardous substances, including asbestos, lead, and radioactive waste. They follow strict protocols to ensure the safety of the environment and public health during the removal process.

Health and Safety Engineers

Aspect	Detail
Hourly Rate	$49.90
Annual Salary	$103,700
Degree Level Required	Bachelor's degree

They identify potential hazards in workplaces and design solutions to prevent accidents and injuries. They develop safety programs, conduct inspections, train employees in safe work practices and ensure compliance with safety regulations.

Healthcare Social Workers

Aspect	Detail
Hourly Rate	$30.3
Annual Salary	$63,000
Degree Level Required	Master's degree

They help patients and their families cope with the social and emotional challenges of illness, injury, or disability. They provide counseling, arrange for support services, connect patients with resources, and advocate for their needs within the healthcare system.

Hearing Aid Specialists

Aspect	Detail
Hourly Rate	$28.2
Annual Salary	$58,700
Degree Level Required	High school diploma or equivalent

They test hearing, fit and adjust hearing aids, and counsel patients with hearing loss. They work to improve patients' communication and quality of life by addressing hearing difficulties.

Heating, Air Conditioning, and Refrigeration Mechanics and Installers

Aspect	Detail
Hourly Rate	$27.5
Annual Salary	$57,300
Degree Level Required	Postsecondary non-degree award

They install, maintain, and repair heating, air conditioning, and refrigeration systems in residential, commercial, and industrial settings. They work with ductwork, thermostats, compressors, and other components of HVAC systems.

Heavy and Tractor-Trailer Truck Drivers

Aspect	Detail
Hourly Rate	$26.2
Annual Salary	$54,400
Degree Level Required	Postsecondary non-degree award

They transport goods over long distances in large trucks. They operate tractor-trailers, load and unload cargo, ensure the secure transport of goods, and maintain logbooks documenting their trips.

Highway Maintenance Workers

Aspect	Detail
Hourly Rate	$22.8
Annual Salary	$47,400
Degree Level Required	High school diploma or equivalent

They maintain the safety and functionality of roads and highways. They repair potholes, clear debris, install signs, paint lines, mow embankments, and may assist with snow and ice removal.

Historians

Aspect	Detail
Hourly Rate	$35
Annual Salary	$72,900
Degree Level Required	Master's degree

They research, analyze, and interpret past events and societies. They examine historical documents, artifacts, and other evidence to reconstruct and understand history. Historians may specialize in specific time periods or regions.

Hoist and Winch Operators

Aspect	Detail
Hourly Rate	$26.9
Annual Salary	$56,000
Degree Level Required	No formal educational credential

They use cranes or other powered lifting equipment to move heavy loads. They operate controls to lift, lower, and position objects in construction, manufacturing, or transportation settings.

Home Appliance Repairers

Aspect	Detail
Hourly Rate	$22.7
Annual Salary	$47,200
Degree Level Required	High school diploma or equivalent

They diagnose and fix problems with washing machines, refrigerators, ovens, and other household appliances. They troubleshoot malfunctions, replace parts, and test appliances to ensure they are working correctly.

Hosts and Hostesses, Restaurant, Lounge, and Coffee Shop

Aspect	Detail
Hourly Rate	$14.1
Annual Salary	$29,300
Degree Level Required	No formal educational credential

They are responsible for greeting customers as they enter the establishment, providing them with menus, and guiding them to their seats. They manage the waitlist, coordinate table settings, and ensure a welcoming atmosphere for guests.

Hotel, Motel, and Resort Desk Clerks

Aspect	Detail
Hourly Rate	$14.8
Annual Salary	$30,800
Degree Level Required	High school diploma or equivalent

They check guests in and out of their accommodations, assign rooms, and respond to guests' requests. They provide information about services, handle reservations, and address any complaints to ensure a pleasant stay for guests.

Human Resources Managers

Aspect	Detail
Hourly Rate	$65.6
Annual Salary	$136,400
Degree Level Required	Bachelor's degree

They plan, direct, and coordinate the administrative functions of an organization. They oversee the recruiting, interviewing, and hiring of new staff; consult with top executives on strategic planning; and serve as a link between an organization's management and its employees.

Human Resources Specialists

Aspect	Detail
Hourly Rate	$32.5
Annual Salary	$67,700
Degree Level Required	Bachelor's degree

They are involved in recruiting, screening, interviewing, and placing workers. They may also handle employee relations, payroll, benefits, and training. They play a key role in matching organizational needs with the skills and abilities of employees.

Hydrologists

Aspect	Detail
Hourly Rate	$42.7
Annual Salary	$88,800
Degree Level Required	Bachelor's degree

They study how water moves across and through the Earth's crust. They use their expertise to solve problems in water quality and availability, including the impact of floods, droughts, and other water-related issues.

Industrial Engineers

Aspect	Detail
Hourly Rate	$47.8
Annual Salary	$99,400
Degree Level Required	Bachelor's degree

They find ways to eliminate wastefulness in production processes. They devise efficient systems that integrate workers, machines, materials, information, and energy to make a product or provide a service.

Industrial Machinery Mechanics

Aspect	Detail
Hourly Rate	$29.6
Annual Salary	$61,500
Degree Level Required	High school diploma or equivalent

They maintain and repair factory equipment and other industrial machinery, such as conveying systems, production machinery, and packaging equipment. They ensure that machines operate safely and efficiently.

Industrial Production Managers

Aspect	Detail
Hourly Rate	$56.3
Annual Salary	$117,000
Degree Level Required	Bachelor's degree

They oversee the daily operations of manufacturing and related plants. They coordinate, plan, and direct the activities used to create a wide range of goods, such as cars, computer equipment, or paper products.

Information Security Analysts

Aspect	Detail
Hourly Rate	$57.9
Annual Salary	$120,400
Degree Level Required	Bachelor's degree

They plan and carry out security measures to protect an organization's computer networks and systems. Their responsibilities are continually expanding as the number of cyberattacks increases.

Insulation Workers, Floor, Ceiling, and Wall

Aspect	Detail
Hourly Rate	$22.9
Annual Salary	$47,600
Degree Level Required	No formal educational credential

They install and replace the materials used to insulate buildings and their mechanical systems to help control and maintain the temperatures in buildings.

Insurance Appraisers, Auto Damage

Aspect	Detail
Hourly Rate	$35.9
Annual Salary	$74,600
Degree Level Required	Postsecondary non-degree award

They inspect cars damaged in accidents to determine repair costs and recommend whether a vehicle can be made safe again. They work for insurance companies to settle claims as quickly and accurately as possible.

Insurance Sales Agents

Aspect	Detail
Hourly Rate	$28.4
Annual Salary	$59,100
Degree Level Required	High school diploma or equivalent

They contact potential customers to sell different types of insurance. Agents explain various insurance policies and help clients choose plans that suit them.

Insurance Underwriters

Aspect	Detail
Hourly Rate	$37.5
Annual Salary	$77,900
Degree Level Required	Bachelor's degree

They evaluate the risk of insuring a home, car, driver, or individual's health or life. They decide whether to provide insurance and under what terms. They evaluate insurance applications and determine coverage amounts and premiums.

Interior Designers

Aspect	Detail
Hourly Rate	$30.1
Annual Salary	$62,600
Degree Level Required	Bachelor's degree

They make indoor spaces functional, safe, and beautiful by determining space requirements and selecting essential and decorative items, such as colors, lighting, and materials. They must be able to draw, read, and edit blueprints.

Interpreters and Translators

Aspect	Detail
Hourly Rate	$27.5
Annual Salary	$57,100
Degree Level Required	Bachelor's degree

They facilitate oral communication between speakers of different languages. They convert spoken words from one language to another in real-time. Translators work with written text, converting documents and other written materials from one language to another.

Janitors and Cleaners, Except Maids and Housekeeping Cleaners

Aspect	Detail
Hourly Rate	$16.9
Annual Salary	$35,100
Degree Level Required	No formal educational credential

They maintain cleanliness and order in commercial, industrial, or institutional buildings. They clean floors, restrooms, offices, and common areas, removing trash, and restocking supplies.

Jewelers and Precious Stone and Metal Workers

Aspect	Detail
Hourly Rate	$22.8
Annual Salary	$47,500
Degree Level Required	High school diploma or equivalent

They design, create, repair and appraise jewelry. They work with precious metals and gemstones, using techniques such as casting, soldering, stone setting, and engraving to produce beautiful and wearable pieces of art.

Judges, Magistrate Judges, and Magistrates

Aspect	Detail
Hourly Rate	$72.61
Annual Salary	$151,000
Degree Level Required	Doctoral or professional degree

They preside over court proceedings, make legal rulings, and issue sentences. Magistrate judges assist judges, overseeing pre-trial matters and handling specific legal cases.

Judicial Law Clerks

Aspect	Detail
Hourly Rate	$27.64
Annual Salary	$57,500
Degree Level Required	Doctoral or professional degree

They provide legal research and support to judges. They analyze cases, draft legal documents, and assist judges in preparing for court proceedings.

Kindergarten Teachers, Except Special Education

Aspect	Detail
Hourly Rate	$30.1
Annual Salary	$62,700
Degree Level Required	Bachelor's degree

They educate young children in the early stages of their academic and social development. They introduce basic concepts in reading, math, science, and social studies, often through play-based learning activities.

Landscape Architects

Aspect	Detail
Hourly Rate	$38.2
Annual Salary	$79,400
Degree Level Required	Bachelor's degree

They design outdoor spaces that are both functional and aesthetically pleasing. They develop plans for parks, gardens, campuses, residential areas, and other outdoor environments, considering factors like topography, vegetation, and environmental impact.

Landscaping and Groundskeeping Workers

Aspect	Detail
Hourly Rate	$18
Annual Salary	$37,400
Degree Level Required	No formal educational credential

They plant and maintain lawns, gardens, trees, and other outdoor areas. They mow, trim, water, fertilize, and may also install hardscapes like walkways and patios.

Laundry and Dry-Cleaning Workers

Aspect	Detail
Hourly Rate	$15
Annual Salary	$31,100
Degree Level Required	No formal educational credential

They clean and press clothing, linens, and other textiles. They may operate washing machines, dryers, ironing equipment, or dry-cleaning machinery.

Law Teachers, Postsecondary

Aspect	Detail
Hourly Rate	$61.3
Annual Salary	$127,400
Degree Level Required	Doctoral or professional degree

They teach courses in various areas of law at colleges and universities. They instruct law students, conduct legal research, and may publish scholarly articles in their field of expertise.

Lawyers

Aspect	Detail
Hourly Rate	$70.1
Annual Salary	$145,800
Degree Level Required	Doctoral or professional degree

They (also called attorneys) provide legal advice to clients and represent them in court. They research laws, prepare legal documents, argue cases, and negotiate settlements. Lawyers may specialize in areas like criminal law, family law, or corporate law.

Legal Secretaries and Administrative Assistants

Aspect	Detail
Hourly Rate	$24.4
Annual Salary	$50,700
Degree Level Required	High school diploma or equivalent

They perform a variety of administrative and clerical tasks to support lawyers and legal executives. Their duties include preparing legal documents, conducting research, and managing schedules, ensuring the efficient operation of legal offices.

Librarians and Media Collections Specialists

Aspect	Detail
Hourly Rate	$31
Annual Salary	$64,400
Degree Level Required	Master's degree

They manage collections of books, periodicals, recordings, and other information resources. They help people find information and conduct research for personal and professional use. Their job is evolving to include more digital resources management.

Lifeguards, Ski Patrol, and Other Protective Service Workers

Aspect	Detail
Hourly Rate	$14.6
Annual Salary	$30,400
Degree Level Required	No formal educational credential

They provide safety services in various environments, such as pools, beaches, and ski resorts. They monitor activities to prevent accidents and provide emergency care in case of injury, ensuring the well-being of participants.

Lighting Technicians

Aspect	Detail
Hourly Rate	$30
Annual Salary	$62,300
Degree Level Required	Postsecondary non-degree award

They set up and control lighting equipment for television, film, theater, and live events. They work closely with directors and designers to create the desired lighting effects, enhancing the overall look of the production.

Loading and Moving Machine Operators, Underground Mining

Aspect	Detail
Hourly Rate	$30.8
Annual Salary	$64,100
Degree Level Required	No formal educational credential

They operate machinery in underground mines to move materials, soil, and rock. They use machines equipped with scoops or shovels to load coal, ore, or rock into transport vehicles or onto conveyors.

Loan Officers

Aspect	Detail
Hourly Rate	$33.7
Annual Salary	$70,000
Degree Level Required	Bachelor's degree

They evaluate, authorize, or recommend approval of loan applications for people and businesses. They assess the financial condition of applicants and determine the likelihood of loans being repaid on time.

Locksmiths and Safe Repairers

Aspect	Detail
Hourly Rate	$23.3
Annual Salary	$48,400
Degree Level Required	High school diploma or equivalent

They install, repair, and open locks; make keys; change locks and safe combinations; and install and repair safes. They provide services to ensure the security of buildings, vehicles, and safes.

Locomotive Engineers

Aspect	Detail
Hourly Rate	$35.85
Annual Salary	$74,600
Degree Level Required	High school diploma or equivalent

They drive passenger or freight trains to destinations. They monitor the train instruments, observe track conditions, and control the speed and braking of the train, ensuring safe and timely arrivals.

Log Graders and Scalers

Aspect	Detail
Hourly Rate	$21.9
Annual Salary	$45,600
Degree Level Required	High school diploma or equivalent

They inspect logs for defects, measure logs to determine their volume, and grade them according to quality standards. This work is crucial for determining the market value and processing requirements of timber.

Logisticians

Aspect	Detail
Hourly Rate	$38.2
Annual Salary	$79,400
Degree Level Required	Bachelor's degree

They analyze and coordinate an organization's supply chain—the system that moves a product from supplier to consumer. They manage the entire life cycle of a product, which includes how a product is acquired, distributed, allocated, and delivered.

Magnetic Resonance Imaging Technologists

Aspect	Detail
Hourly Rate	$40.3
Annual Salary	$83,800
Degree Level Required	Associate's degree

They operate MRI scanners to create diagnostic images. They prepare patients for procedures, explaining the process and ensuring patient safety, and adjust the scanner to optimize the image quality.

Maids and Housekeeping Cleaners

Aspect	Detail
Hourly Rate	$16.1
Annual Salary	$33,500
Degree Level Required	No formal educational credential

They perform cleaning duties to maintain private households or commercial establishments, such as hotels and hospitals, in a clean and orderly manner. Tasks may include cleaning rooms, hallways, and other living or work areas.

Mail Clerks and Mail Machine Operators, Except Postal Service

Aspect	Detail
Hourly Rate	$17.7
Annual Salary	$36,900
Degree Level Required	High school diploma or equivalent

They prepare outgoing mail and manage incoming mail. They operate machines that collate, fold, and insert documents into envelopes for mailing. They also ensure the correct postage is applied to outgoing mail.

Maintenance Workers, Machinery

Aspect	Detail
Hourly Rate	$27.6
Annual Salary	$57,400
Degree Level Required	High school diploma or equivalent

They maintain and repair factory equipment and other industrial machinery, such as conveying systems, production machinery, and packaging equipment. They ensure machinery operates efficiently and safely, performing routine maintenance and troubleshooting problems.

Makeup Artists, Theatrical and Performance

Aspect	Detail
Hourly Rate	$22.8
Annual Salary	$47,400
Degree Level Required	Postsecondary non-degree award

They specialize in applying makeup to performers for stage productions, film, television, and other live events. They create character looks, enhance features, apply prosthetics or special effects makeup, and ensure makeup is suitable for stage lighting and camera work.

Management Analysts

Aspect	Detail
Hourly Rate	$47.8
Annual Salary	$99,500
Degree Level Required	Bachelor's degree

They often referred to as management consultants, help organizations improve efficiency and solve problems. They analyze business operations, identify areas for improvement, and recommend solutions or strategies to enhance performance.

Manicurists and Pedicurists

Aspect	Detail
Hourly Rate	$16.5
Annual Salary	$34,300
Degree Level Required	Postsecondary non-degree award

They provide nail care services including cleaning, shaping, and polishing fingernails and toenails. They may also apply artificial nails, provide hand or foot massages, and offer nail art.

Marine Engineers and Naval Architects

Aspect	Detail
Hourly Rate	$48.2
Annual Salary	$100,300
Degree Level Required	Bachelor's degree

They design, build, and maintain the propulsion systems and other mechanical and electrical equipment on ships, boats, and submarines. Naval architects are responsible for the overall design of a ship, including its hull shape, stability, and layout.

Market Research Analysts and Marketing Specialists

Aspect	Detail
Hourly Rate	$35.9
Annual Salary	$74,700
Degree Level Required	Bachelor's degree

They study market conditions to examine potential sales of products or services. They gather data on consumer demographics, preferences, and buying habits, and help businesses develop effective marketing strategies.

Marketing Managers

Aspect	Detail
Hourly Rate	$75.8
Annual Salary	$157,700
Degree Level Required	Bachelor's degree

They develop and oversee an organization's marketing campaigns. They set marketing goals, manage budgets, create promotional strategies, and track the success of marketing efforts across various media channels.

Marriage and Family Therapists

Aspect	Detail
Hourly Rate	$28.2
Annual Salary	$58,600
Degree Level Required	Master's degree

They provide counseling to couples, families, and individuals to address relationship problems and mental health concerns within a family context. They help clients improve communication, resolve conflicts, and develop healthier relationship patterns.

Massage Therapists

Aspect	Detail
Hourly Rate	$26.6
Annual Salary	$55,400
Degree Level Required	Postsecondary non-degree award

They manipulate muscles and soft tissues of the body to relieve pain, reduce stress, promote relaxation, and improve overall well-being. They use various massage techniques and may specialize in specific modalities.

Materials Engineers

Aspect	Detail
Hourly Rate	$50
Annual Salary	$104,100
Degree Level Required	Bachelor's degree

They develop, process, and test materials used to create a wide range of products. They analyze the properties of metals, ceramics, polymers, and composites, and find applications for new materials.

Mathematical Science Teachers, Postsecondary

Aspect	Detail
Hourly Rate	$39
Annual Salary	$81,100
Degree Level Required	Doctoral or professional degree

They teach courses in mathematics, statistics, or other mathematical sciences at colleges and universities. They instruct students in advanced mathematical concepts, conduct research, and may publish scholarly works.

Mathematicians

Aspect	Detail
Hourly Rate	$56
Annual Salary	$116,500
Degree Level Required	Master's degree

They use advanced analytical techniques to develop and apply mathematical theories. They may work in pure mathematics, focusing on theoretical concepts, or applied mathematics, using math to solve problems in fields like science, engineering, and business.

Meat, Poultry, and Fish Cutters and Trimmers

Aspect	Detail
Hourly Rate	$17.5
Annual Salary	$36,300
Degree Level Required	No formal educational credential

They cut, trim, and prepare meat, poultry, and fish for retail or wholesale. They use knives, saws, and specialized equipment to separate cuts, debone, and prepare products for sale.

Mechanical Engineers

Aspect	Detail
Hourly Rate	$47.9
Annual Salary	$99,600
Degree Level Required	Bachelor's degree

They design, develop, build, and test mechanical devices, including tools, engines, and machines. They work in an array of industries, creating products and systems for heating and cooling, manufacturing, power generation, and more.

Medical Dosimetrists

Aspect	Detail
Hourly Rate	$63.9
Annual Salary	$132,900
Degree Level Required	Bachelor's degree

They work with radiation oncologists to develop radiation treatment plans. They calculate the precise dose and distribution of radiation needed for each patient's cancer treatment, ensuring safety and effectiveness.

Medical Equipment Repairers

Aspect	Detail
Hourly Rate	$29.2
Annual Salary	$60,700
Degree Level Required	Associate's degree

They install, maintain, repair, and calibrate medical equipment such as diagnostic imaging machines, patient monitors, and life support systems. They work in hospitals, clinics, and other healthcare settings.

Medical Secretaries and Administrative Assistants

Aspect	Detail
Hourly Rate	$19.6
Annual Salary	$40,700
Degree Level Required	High school diploma or equivalent

They support the administrative functions in healthcare settings. They schedule appointments, maintain medical records, handle insurance billing, and perform other tasks to keep the office running smoothly.

Medical Transcriptionists

Aspect	Detail
Hourly Rate	$17.8
Annual Salary	$37,100
Degree Level Required	Postsecondary non-degree award

They listen to voice recordings from doctors and other healthcare providers, transcribing them into written medical reports, notes, and other documentation.

Meeting, Convention, and Event Planners

Aspect	Detail
Hourly Rate	$27.4
Annual Salary	$57,000
Degree Level Required	Bachelor's degree

They coordinate all aspects of events like conferences, meetings, trade shows, and special occasions. They manage logistics such as venue selection, catering, transportation, audio-visual setup, and speaker arrangements.

Mental Health and Substance Abuse Social Workers

Aspect	Detail
Hourly Rate	$26.9
Annual Salary	$56,000
Degree Level Required	Master's degree

They assist individuals living with mental health conditions, addiction, or other behavioral issues. They provide counseling, connect clients to resources, advocate for their needs, and help them develop coping skills.

Microbiologists

Aspect	Detail
Hourly Rate	$41.1
Annual Salary	$85,500
Degree Level Required	Bachelor's degree

They study microorganisms such as bacteria, viruses, fungi, and parasites. They research their characteristics, how they interact with the environment, and their impact on human, animal, and plant health.

Middle School Teachers

Aspect	Detail
Hourly Rate	$30.9
Annual Salary	$64,300
Degree Level Required	Bachelor's degree

They educate students typically in grades 6-8. They teach a variety of subjects, manage larger class sizes, and help students transition between the structures of elementary and high school.

Millwrights

Aspect	Detail
Hourly Rate	$30.3
Annual Salary	$63,000
Degree Level Required	High school diploma or equivalent

They install, maintain, repair, and dismantle heavy industrial machinery in factories, power plants, and other industrial settings. They work with precision tools and must have a strong understanding of mechanics and blueprints.

Mining and Geological Engineers

Aspect	Detail
Hourly Rate	$48.4
Annual Salary	$100,700
Degree Level Required	Bachelor's degree

They design safe and efficient mines to extract minerals, metals, and other natural resources. They plan mine layouts, ventilation systems, transportation, assess geological factors, and ensure environmental regulations are met.

Model Makers, Metal and Plastic

Aspect	Detail
Hourly Rate	$30.9
Annual Salary	$64,200
Degree Level Required	High school diploma or equivalent

They create precise models of products, prototypes, or parts for manufacturing using metal, plastic, and other materials. Their models help test designs, visualize products, and support the manufacturing process.

Models

Aspect	Detail
Hourly Rate	$22.8
Annual Salary	$47,500
Degree Level Required	No formal educational credential

They showcase clothing or other products in fashion shows, advertisements, and for artists or photographers. They pose and move according to the needs of the photographer, fashion designer, or client.

Molders, Shapers, and Casters, Except Metal and Plastic

Aspect	Detail
Hourly Rate	$20.9
Annual Salary	$43,400
Degree Level Required	High school diploma or equivalent

They work with a variety of materials such as clay, glass, concrete, and stone to create sculptures, parts, and products. They use molds, forms, or their hands to shape materials into the desired forms, often in art, manufacturing, or construction applications.

Morticians, Undertakers, and Funeral Arrangers

Aspect	Detail
Hourly Rate	$24.6
Annual Salary	$51,100
Degree Level Required	Associate's degree

They provide services for the deceased and their families. Morticians and undertakers prepare bodies for burial or cremation and organize the details of funerals. Funeral arrangers work closely with families to plan the various aspects of funeral services, including the ceremony, transportation of the body, and filing of legal documents.

Motion Picture Projectionists

Aspect	Detail
Hourly Rate	$16.9
Annual Salary	$35,200
Degree Level Required	No formal educational credential

They set up and operate film projection and related sound reproduction equipment. They are responsible for loading digital or film projects, ensuring that movies are displayed correctly, and maintaining the equipment used in movie theaters.

Motorboat Operators

Aspect	Detail
Hourly Rate	$22.4
Annual Salary	$46,500
Degree Level Required	Postsecondary non-degree award

They navigate boats with motors for various purposes, including fishing, tours, and transportation. They must understand navigation, safety procedures, and maintenance of their vessels to ensure safe and efficient operation.

Motorcycle Mechanics

Aspect	Detail
Hourly Rate	$22.3
Annual Salary	$46,300
Degree Level Required	Postsecondary non-degree award

They specialize in repairing and maintaining motorcycles, scooters, mopeds, and sometimes other power sport vehicles. They work on engines, transmissions, brakes, and electrical systems, and must stay updated with evolving technology in the industry.

Museum Technicians and Conservators

Aspect	Detail
Hourly Rate	$23.4
Annual Salary	$48,700
Degree Level Required	Bachelor's degree

They work to preserve and restore artifacts, works of art, and specimens. Conservators focus on the care and treatment of these items, while technicians prepare and maintain exhibits. Both roles are critical in preserving historical and cultural objects for future generations.

Music Directors and Composers

Aspect	Detail
Hourly Rate	$30.1
Annual Salary	$62,600
Degree Level Required	Bachelor's degree

They write, arrange, and conduct musical performances. Music directors lead orchestras, choirs, and other musical groups, while composers create original music that is performed by musicians or electronic media.

Musical Instrument Repairers and Tuners

Aspect	Detail
Hourly Rate	$18.34
Annual Salary	$38,200
Degree Level Required	High school diploma or equivalent

They specialize in maintaining and repairing instruments to ensure they produce the correct sound. Their work includes tuning instruments to the right pitch, replacing parts, and adjusting mechanisms.

Musicians and Singers

Aspect	Detail
Hourly Rate	$39.14
Annual Salary	$81,400
Degree Level Required	No formal educational credential

They perform music for live audiences and recordings. They may play instruments, sing, or do both, often specializing in a particular genre of music. Their careers require talent, practice, and often, formal training in music.

Natural Sciences Managers

Aspect	Detail
Hourly Rate	$75.9
Annual Salary	$157,800
Degree Level Required	Bachelor's degree

They oversee the work of scientists in fields such as biology, chemistry, and physics. They plan and direct studies and research projects, manage budgets, and coordinate activities between their department and other organizations.

Network and Computer Systems Administrators

Aspect	Detail
Hourly Rate	$45.9
Annual Salary	$95,400
Degree Level Required	Bachelor's degree

They are responsible for the day-to-day operation of an organization's computer networks. They install, support, and manage the networks and computer systems that keep information flowing. They ensure networks are secure and up-to-date.

Neurologists

Aspect	Detail
Hourly Rate	$107.82
Annual Salary	$224,300
Degree Level Required	Doctoral or professional degree

They are physicians who specialize in diagnosing and treating disorders of the nervous system, including the brain, spinal cord, and nerves. They manage conditions such as epilepsy, stroke, multiple sclerosis, and Parkinson's disease.

News Analysts, Reporters, and Journalists

Aspect	Detail
Hourly Rate	$26.90
Annual Salary	$56,000
Degree Level Required	Bachelor's degree

They gather information, conduct interviews, and write news stories for print, broadcast, or online media. Reporters cover local, national, or international events, while analysts offer commentary and interpretation of news.

Nuclear Engineers

Aspect	Detail
Hourly Rate	$60.3
Annual Salary	$125,500
Degree Level Required	Bachelor's degree

They research and develop the processes, systems, and instruments used to harness nuclear energy and radiation. They design nuclear power plants, nuclear equipment, and may focus on safe radioactive waste disposal.

Nuclear Medicine Technologists

Aspect	Detail
Hourly Rate	$44.5
Annual Salary	$92,500
Degree Level Required	Associate's degree

They prepare and administer radioactive substances (radiopharmaceuticals) to patients for diagnostic imaging or therapeutic treatments. They operate specialized imaging equipment and ensure patient safety.

Nuclear Power Reactor Operators

Aspect	Detail
Hourly Rate	$57.9
Annual Salary	$120,400
Degree Level Required	High school diploma or equivalent

They control and monitor nuclear reactors in power plants. They adjust control rods, manage power levels, respond to emergencies, and ensure the safe and efficient operation of reactors.

Nurse Anesthetists

Aspect	Detail
Hourly Rate	$102.3
Annual Salary	$212,700
Degree Level Required	Master's degree

They administer anesthesia to patients during surgery or other medical procedures. They assess patients, monitor vital signs, manage dosages, and address any complications related to anesthesia.

Nurse Midwives

Aspect	Detail
Hourly Rate	$62.4
Annual Salary	$129,700
Degree Level Required	Master's degree

They are advanced practice nurses who provide primary care to women throughout their lives, with a focus on pregnancy, childbirth, and postpartum care. They also offer gynecological, and family planning services.

Nurse Practitioners

Aspect	Detail
Hourly Rate	$60.7
Annual Salary	$126,300
Degree Level Required	Master's degree

They are advanced practice nurses who provide primary and specialty healthcare. They diagnose illnesses, prescribe medications, order and interpret tests, and manage patients' overall healthcare.

Nursing Assistants

Aspect	Detail
Hourly Rate	$18.4
Annual Salary	$38,200
Degree Level Required	Postsecondary non-degree award

They provide basic care to patients in hospitals, nursing homes, and other healthcare settings. They assist with activities of daily living like bathing, dressing, and eating, and monitor patients' vital signs.

Obstetricians and Gynecologists

Aspect	Detail
Hourly Rate	$117.8
Annual Salary	$245,000
Degree Level Required	Doctoral or professional degree

They often called OB/GYNs, provide specialized medical care related to the female reproductive system. Obstetricians manage pregnancy, childbirth, and postpartum care. Gynecologists focus on women's reproductive health issues.

Occupational Therapists

Aspect	Detail
Hourly Rate	$46.3
Annual Salary	$96,400
Degree Level Required	Master's degree

They help people of all ages who have physical, sensory, or cognitive challenges develop, recover, or maintain daily living and work skills. They design and implement therapy programs to enhance patients' independence and function.

Operations Research Analysts

Aspect	Detail
Hourly Rate	$40.2
Annual Salary	$83,700
Degree Level Required	Bachelor's degree

They use mathematical and analytical methods to help organizations investigate complex issues, identify and solve problems, and make better decisions. They apply optimization, data mining, and statistical analysis to formulate and solve problems in logistics, business, healthcare, and other fields.

Ophthalmologists, Except Pediatric

Aspect	Detail
Hourly Rate	$105.8
Annual Salary	$220,000
Degree Level Required	Doctoral or professional degree

They are medical doctors specializing in eye and vision care, diagnosing and treating eye diseases, conducting eye surgeries, and prescribing and fitting eyeglasses and contact lenses. Their focus excludes the specialized treatment of children, which is handled by pediatric ophthalmologists.

Optometrists

Aspect	Detail
Hourly Rate	$63.4
Annual Salary	$131,900
Degree Level Required	Doctoral or professional degree

They examine the eyes and other parts of the visual system. They diagnose and treat visual problems and manage diseases, injuries, and other disorders of the eyes. They prescribe eyeglasses or contact lenses as needed.

Oral and Maxillofacial Surgeons

Aspect	Detail
Hourly Rate	$129.8
Annual Salary	$270,000
Degree Level Required	Doctoral or professional degree

They specialize in surgery on the face, mouth, and jaws. They perform procedures such as tooth extractions, corrective jaw surgery, and treatment of facial trauma, pathologies, and deformities.

Orthodontists

Aspect	Detail
Hourly Rate	$84.3
Annual Salary	$175,300
Degree Level Required	Doctoral or professional degree

They specialize in diagnosing, preventing, and treating dental and facial irregularities. They design and fabricate appliances, such as braces and aligners, to straighten teeth and improve bite function.

Orthopedic Surgeons, Except Pediatric

Aspect	Detail
Hourly Rate	$132.2
Annual Salary	$275,000
Degree Level Required	Doctoral or professional degree

They focus on the diagnosis, treatment, prevention, and rehabilitation of injuries, disorders, and diseases of the body's musculoskeletal system. This includes bones, joints, ligaments, muscles, and tendons. They work with all age groups except children, which is a specialization within orthopedics.

Orthotists and Prosthetists

Aspect	Detail
Hourly Rate	$37.8
Annual Salary	$78,100
Degree Level Required	Master's degree

They design and fit medical supportive devices, such as braces and artificial limbs. Orthotists specialize in orthopedic braces, while prosthetists specialize in prosthetic limbs, working with patients who have disabilities or injuries.

Packers and Packagers, Hand

Aspect	Detail
Hourly Rate	$16.8
Annual Salary	$34,900
Degree Level Required	No formal educational credential

They pack or package by hand a wide variety of products and materials. This includes wrapping, boxing, bottling, and labeling products in preparation for shipping and distribution.

Painters, Construction and Maintenance

Aspect	Detail
Hourly Rate	$22.9
Annual Salary	$47,700
Degree Level Required	No formal educational credential

They apply paint, stain, and coatings to walls, buildings, bridges, and other structures. They perform tasks ranging from simple touch-ups to complete renovations, working to protect surfaces and improve appearance.

Paperhangers

Aspect	Detail
Hourly Rate	$23.3
Annual Salary	$48,500
Degree Level Required	No formal educational credential

They apply wallpaper and fabric coverings to walls and ceilings. They must measure, cut, and apply these materials carefully to ensure smooth and properly aligned surfaces.

Paralegals and Legal Assistants

Aspect	Detail
Hourly Rate	$29.3
Annual Salary	$61,000
Degree Level Required	Associate's degree

They support lawyers by performing a variety of tasks, including conducting legal research, organizing and maintaining documents, and drafting legal documents. They help prepare for hearings, trials, and corporate meetings.

Paramedics

Aspect	Detail
Hourly Rate	$25.6
Annual Salary	$53,200
Degree Level Required	Postsecondary non-degree award

They provide advanced medical care to patients in emergency situations. They respond to emergency calls, perform medical services, and transport patients to medical facilities. They are trained to manage respiratory, trauma, and cardiac emergencies.

Parking Enforcement Workers

Aspect	Detail
Hourly Rate	$22.5
Annual Salary	$46,900
Degree Level Required	High school diploma or equivalent

They patrol assigned areas to enforce parking ordinances. They issue tickets for parking violations, arrange for towing of vehicles, and may collect parking fees.

Parts Salespersons

Aspect	Detail
Hourly Rate	$17.7
Annual Salary	$36,900
Degree Level Required	No formal educational credential

They sell spare and replacement parts and equipment, especially car parts. They advise customers on the use and care of parts and may work in parts departments of auto dealerships, retail stores, or wholesale warehouses.

Paving, Surfacing, and Tamping Equipment Operators

Aspect	Detail
Hourly Rate	$23.6
Annual Salary	$49,000
Degree Level Required	High school diploma or equivalent

They operate equipment used to spread, smooth, level, or steel-reinforce stone, concrete, or asphalt on road beds, parking lots, or airport runways and taxiways. They handle machines like paving and surfacing equipment to create smooth and durable surfaces.

Pediatric Surgeons

Aspect	Detail
Hourly Rate	$161.1
Annual Salary	$335,100
Degree Level Required	Doctoral or professional degree

They are specialized surgeons who focus on the diagnosis, operative, and postoperative management of surgical problems in children, including infants, children, adolescents, and young adults. They perform surgeries to correct or treat various conditions, diseases, and injuries in young patients.

Pediatricians, General

Aspect	Detail
Hourly Rate	$95.5
Annual Salary	$198,700
Degree Level Required	Doctoral or professional degree

They are doctors who specialize in the physical, emotional, and social health of children from birth to young adulthood. They focus on preventive health maintenance and medical care for children who are acutely or chronically ill.

Personal Financial Advisors

Aspect	Detail
Hourly Rate	$47.9
Annual Salary	$99,600
Degree Level Required	Bachelor's degree

They provide advice on financial matters to individuals. They help with investments, taxes, estate planning, college savings accounts, insurance, mortgages, and retirement, among other things, to manage clients' financial objectives.

Pest Control Workers

Aspect	Detail
Hourly Rate	$20.9
Annual Salary	$43,500
Degree Level Required	High school diploma or equivalent

They inspect properties for evidence of infestations and use a mix of natural and chemical treatments to control pests like insects and rodents. They advise clients on how to prevent future infestations.

Petroleum Engineers

Aspect	Detail
Hourly Rate	$65.2
Annual Salary	$135,700
Degree Level Required	Bachelor's degree

They devise methods to improve oil and gas extraction and production. They design equipment and processes to achieve the maximum profitable recovery of oil and gas. This might involve the use of new techniques to extract oil from old wells or the development of new drilling equipment.

Petroleum Pump System Operators

Aspect	Detail
Hourly Rate	$45.5
Annual Salary	$94,600
Degree Level Required	High school diploma or equivalent

They manage and operate systems that pump petroleum products through pipelines. They monitor the movement of products through pipelines or into and out of tanks, adjusting valves and equipment to manage flow and maintain schedules.

Pharmacists

Aspect	Detail
Hourly Rate	$65.4
Annual Salary	$136,100
Degree Level Required	Doctoral or professional degree

They dispense prescription medications to patients and offer expertise in the safe use of prescriptions. They may also provide advice on how to lead a healthy lifestyle, conduct health and wellness screenings, provide immunizations, and oversee the medications given to patients.

Pharmacy Technicians

Aspect	Detail
Hourly Rate	$19.4
Annual Salary	$40,300
Degree Level Required	High school diploma or equivalent

They assist pharmacists in dispensing prescription medication to customers or health professionals. They may measure, mix, count out, label, and record amounts and dosages of medications according to prescription orders.

Photographers

Aspect	Detail
Hourly Rate	$19.6
Annual Salary	$40,800
Degree Level Required	High school diploma or equivalent

They use cameras to capture images to tell stories, document events, or create art. They may specialize in various types of photography, such as portrait, commercial, news, or fine arts photography.

Physical Therapists

Aspect	Detail
Hourly Rate	$48
Annual Salary	$99,800
Degree Level Required	Doctoral or professional degree

They help patients reduce pain and improve or restore mobility through physical rehabilitation techniques, exercises, and treatments. They work with patients who have injuries, disabilities, or chronic conditions.

Physician Assistants

Aspect	Detail
Hourly Rate	$62.5
Annual Salary	$130,100
Degree Level Required	Master's degree

They practice medicine on teams with physicians, surgeons, and other healthcare workers. They examine, diagnose, and treat patients under a physician's supervision and may also prescribe medication.

Physicians, Pathologists

Aspect	Detail
Hourly Rate	$120.3
Annual Salary	$250,200
Degree Level Required	Doctoral or professional degree

They diagnose and study diseases and conditions by examining body tissues, fluids, and organs. They play a critical role in health care, often determining the cause of death or the nature of diseases by performing laboratory tests and biopsies.

Physicists

Aspect	Detail
Hourly Rate	$74.9
Annual Salary	$155,700
Degree Level Required	Doctoral or professional degree

They study the properties of matter, energy, and the universe. They conduct experiments and use mathematical models to understand the laws of nature, from the largest galaxies to the smallest particles.

Pile Driver Operators

Aspect	Detail
Hourly Rate	$30.6
Annual Salary	$63,600
Degree Level Required	High school diploma or equivalent

They use specialized machinery to drive piles (long beams of wood, steel, or concrete) deep into the ground to provide foundation support for buildings, bridges, and other structures.

Pipelayers

Aspect	Detail
Hourly Rate	$22.8
Annual Salary	$47,400
Degree Level Required	No formal educational credential

They lay and connect sections of pipe for water, sewer, oil, gas, or other systems. They cut pipe sections, dig trenches, align and join pipe, and test for leaks.

Plasterers and Stucco Masons

Aspect	Detail
Hourly Rate	$25.3
Annual Salary	$52,700
Degree Level Required	No formal educational credential

They apply plaster to interior walls, ceilings, and partitions to create smooth, finished surfaces. Stucco masons apply a similar material (stucco) to exterior surfaces for a decorative and protective finish.

Plating Machine Operators, Metal and Plastic

Aspect	Detail
Hourly Rate	$19.1
Annual Salary	$39,800
Degree Level Required	High school diploma or equivalent

They use machines to coat metal or plastic parts with a layer of another metal for decorative or protective purposes. They load parts, monitor the plating process, and ensure quality.

Plumbers, Pipefitters, and Steamfitters

Aspect	Detail
Hourly Rate	$29.6
Annual Salary	$61,600
Degree Level Required	High school diploma or equivalent

They install and repair pipe systems that carry water, steam, gas, or other fluids in residential, commercial, and industrial settings.

Podiatrists

Aspect	Detail
Hourly Rate	$68.1
Annual Salary	$141,700
Degree Level Required	Doctoral or professional degree

They are specialized medical doctors who diagnose and treat conditions of the foot, ankle, and lower leg. They address issues like injuries, infections, deformities, and diseases related to the feet.

Police and Sheriff's Patrol Officers

Aspect	Detail
Hourly Rate	$34.8
Annual Salary	$72,300
Degree Level Required	High school diploma or equivalent

They protect lives and property. They enforce laws, make arrests, investigate crimes, respond to emergencies, and maintain public order.

Political Scientists

Aspect	Detail
Hourly Rate	$63.7
Annual Salary	$132,400
Degree Level Required	Master's degree

They study political systems, structures, and behaviors. They analyze government policies, political trends, and the impact of political events, often specializing in fields like international relations or public policy.

Postal Service Clerks

Aspect	Detail
Hourly Rate	$28.7
Annual Salary	$59,600
Degree Level Required	No formal educational credential

They process mail, sell stamps and postal products, and provide customer service in post offices. They sort mail, operate mail processing equipment, and handle customer transactions.

Postal Service Mail Carriers

Aspect	Detail
Hourly Rate	$27.1
Annual Salary	$56,400
Degree Level Required	No formal educational credential

They carriers deliver and collect mail along assigned routes on foot or by vehicle. They sort mail, prepare it for delivery, and interact with customers along their routes.

Postmasters and Mail Superintendents

Aspect	Detail
Hourly Rate	$42.6
Annual Salary	$88,700
Degree Level Required	High school diploma or equivalent

They oversee the operations of post offices or mail distribution centers. They manage staff, budgets, mail processing, and ensure the efficient delivery of mail.

Pourers and Casters, Metal

Aspect	Detail
Hourly Rate	$23.4
Annual Salary	$48,700
Degree Level Required	High school diploma or equivalent

They melt and pour molten metal into molds to create metal castings. They operate furnaces, prepare molds, and monitor the casting process to ensure the quality of finished products.

Power Distributors and Dispatchers

Aspect	Detail
Hourly Rate	$50.4
Annual Salary	$104,800
Degree Level Required	High school diploma or equivalent

They control the flow of electricity from power plants to substations and users. They monitor current converters, voltage transformers, and circuit breakers over a network of transmission and distribution lines.

Power Plant Operators

Aspect	Detail
Hourly Rate	$46.7
Annual Salary	$97,100
Degree Level Required	High school diploma or equivalent

They manage the systems that generate and distribute electric power. They control the boilers, turbines, generators, and auxiliary equipment in power-generating plants to ensure efficient and safe operation.

Prepress Technicians and Workers

Aspect	Detail
Hourly Rate	$21.7
Annual Salary	$45,100
Degree Level Required	Postsecondary non-degree award

They prepare text and images for printing in commercial and digital presses. They edit graphics, convert images, and may create proofs for review before printing begins to ensure accuracy and quality.

Printing Press Operators

Aspect	Detail
Hourly Rate	$20.1
Annual Salary	$41,900
Degree Level Required	High school diploma or equivalent

They run and maintain the machines that print newspapers, books, magazines, and other materials. They set up the press, make adjustments during the printing process, and perform routine maintenance on the equipment.

Private Detectives and Investigators

Aspect	Detail
Hourly Rate	$23.8
Annual Salary	$49,600
Degree Level Required	High school diploma or equivalent

They search for information about legal, financial, and personal matters. They offer many services, such as verifying people's backgrounds, tracing missing persons, and investigating computer crimes.

Probation Officers and Correctional Treatment Specialists

Aspect	Detail
Hourly Rate	$29.7
Annual Salary	$61,800
Degree Level Required	Bachelor's degree

They provide social services to assist in rehabilitation of law offenders in custody or on probation or parole. They develop rehabilitation plans and supervise offenders' activities to prevent them from committing new crimes.

Procurement Clerks

Aspect	Detail
Hourly Rate	$22.5
Annual Salary	$46,700
Degree Level Required	High school diploma or equivalent

They handle the acquisition of products and services for their organization. They prepare purchase orders, solicit bid proposals, and review requisitions for goods and services.

Producers and Directors

Aspect	Detail
Hourly Rate	$39.7
Annual Salary	$82,600
Degree Level Required	Bachelor's degree

They create motion pictures, television shows, live theater, commercials, and other performing arts productions. They interpret scripts, oversee creative aspects, and manage financial decisions to bring a project to completion.

Project Management Specialists

Aspect	Detail
Hourly Rate	$47.4
Annual Salary	$98,600
Degree Level Required	Bachelor's degree

They plan, initiate, and manage projects, leading teams toward achieving goals within constraints such as time, cost, and scope. They work across various industries, ensuring projects proceed efficiently and effectively.

Proofreaders and Copy Markers

Aspect	Detail
Hourly Rate	$23.5
Annual Salary	$48,800
Degree Level Required	Bachelor's degree

They read transcripts and written material to detect and correct errors in text, grammar, and punctuation. They ensure the accuracy and consistency of written documents before publication.

Property Appraisers and Assessors

Aspect	Detail
Hourly Rate	$29.7
Annual Salary	$61,700
Degree Level Required	Bachelor's degree

They determine the value of properties for the purpose of taxation, investment, or sale. They inspect properties, review similar property sales, and assess property values based on their findings.

Property, Real Estate, and Community Association Managers

Aspect	Detail
Hourly Rate	$30.2
Annual Salary	$62,900
Degree Level Required	High school diploma or equivalent

They take care of the many aspects of residential, commercial, or industrial properties. They ensure the property is well-maintained, has a nice appearance, and preserves its resale or leasing value.

Psychiatrists

Aspect	Detail
Hourly Rate	$109.08
Annual Salary	$226,900
Degree Level Required	Doctoral or professional degree

They are medical doctors who diagnose, treat, and help prevent disorders of the mind. They prescribe medication, conduct physical exams, and may also provide psychotherapy.

Public Relations Managers

Aspect	Detail
Hourly Rate	$62.23
Annual Salary	$129,400
Degree Level Required	Bachelor's degree

They plan and direct the creation of material that will maintain or enhance the public image of their employer or client. They craft media releases and develop social media programs to shape public perception and increase awareness of their organization's work and goals.

Public Safety Telecommunicators

Aspect	Detail
Hourly Rate	$23.5
Annual Salary	$48,900
Degree Level Required	High school diploma or equivalent

They answer emergency calls (911) and dispatch police, fire, or ambulance services. They gather information from callers, prioritize calls, communicate with emergency responders, and provide instructions to callers in crisis situations.

Pump Operators, Except Wellhead Pumpers

Aspect	Detail
Hourly Rate	$26.3
Annual Salary	$54,700
Degree Level Required	High school diploma or equivalent

They control and monitor pumps that move liquids or gases like oil, chemicals, or water through pipelines, refineries, or other industrial systems. They ensure proper flow rates, pressures, and temperatures.

Purchasing Managers

Aspect	Detail
Hourly Rate	$65.6
Annual Salary	$136,400
Degree Level Required	Bachelor's degree

They oversee the procurement of goods and services for organizations at the best possible prices and terms. They manage suppliers, negotiate contracts, and ensure organizations have the resources they need to operate.

Radiation Therapists

Aspect	Detail
Hourly Rate	$47.3
Annual Salary	$98,300
Degree Level Required	Associate's degree

They administer radiation treatments, often to cancer patients, following precise plans developed by radiation oncologists. They position patients, operate radiation equipment, monitor safety, and provide patient support.

Radio, Cellular, and Tower Equipment Installers and Repairers

Aspect	Detail
Hourly Rate	$29.5
Annual Salary	$61,400
Degree Level Required	Associate's degree

They install, maintain, and repair telecommunications equipment such as radio antennas, transmitters, cell towers, and related infrastructure. They work at heights and with complex systems to ensure reliable communication networks.

Radiologic Technologists and Technicians

Aspect	Detail
Hourly Rate	$35.3
Annual Salary	$73,500
Degree Level Required	Associate's degree

They perform medical imaging procedures like X-rays, CT scans, and MRI scans. They position patients, operate imaging equipment, follow safety protocols, and produce images used by doctors for diagnosis.

Radiologists

Aspect	Detail
Hourly Rate	$125.2
Annual Salary	$260,400
Degree Level Required	Doctoral or professional degree

They are specialized medical doctors who interpret diagnostic images like X-rays, CT scans, MRIs, and ultrasounds. They analyze these images to identify abnormalities, diagnose diseases, and guide treatment.

Rail Car Repairers

Aspect	Detail
Hourly Rate	$31.3
Annual Salary	$65,100
Degree Level Required	High school diploma or equivalent

They inspect, maintain, and repair railroad freight and passenger cars. They fix brakes, wheels, car bodies, and other components, often using welding and other specialized techniques.

Rail Yard Engineers, Dinkey Operators, and Hostlers

Aspect	Detail
Hourly Rate	$27.5
Annual Salary	$57,100
Degree Level Required	High school diploma or equivalent

They operate small locomotives that move railcars around rail yards, assembling them into trains or positioning them for loading or unloading.

Railroad Brake, Signal, and Switch Operators and Locomotive Firers

Aspect	Detail
Hourly Rate	$30.6
Annual Salary	$63,600
Degree Level Required	High school diploma or equivalent

They perform various critical tasks in railroad operation. Brake operators ensure the proper function of train braking systems. Signal & switch operators control track switches and signals. Locomotive firers used to monitor steam engine boilers, but have a less prominent role in modern trains.

Railroad Conductors and Yardmasters

Aspect	Detail
Hourly Rate	$34.2
Annual Salary	$71,200
Degree Level Required	High school diploma or equivalent

They oversee the operation of trains, making sure schedules are followed, cargo is secure, and safety regulations are adhered to. Yardmasters coordinate the activities of rail yards, directing the movement and placement of railcars.

Rail-Track Laying and Maintenance Equipment Operators

Aspect	Detail
Hourly Rate	$32.2
Annual Salary	$67,000
Degree Level Required	High school diploma or equivalent

They operate specialized machinery to install, maintain, and repair railroad tracks. They use equipment to lay rails, replace ties, surface ballast, and ensure the safe operation of rail lines.

Real Estate Sales Agents

Aspect	Detail
Hourly Rate	$26.1
Annual Salary	$54,300
Degree Level Required	High school diploma or equivalent

They assist clients with buying and selling residential or commercial properties. They list properties, show homes, negotiate offers, and facilitate the closing process.

Receptionists and Information Clerks

Aspect	Detail
Hourly Rate	$17.3
Annual Salary	$35,900
Degree Level Required	High school diploma or equivalent

They greet visitors and answer phones, often serving as the first point of contact for an organization. They provide information and direct visitors to their destinations within the facility.

Recreation Workers

Aspect	Detail
Hourly Rate	$16.6
Annual Salary	$34,500
Degree Level Required	High school diploma or equivalent

They design and lead activities to help people stay active, improve fitness, and have fun. They work in parks, recreation facilities, camps, and other settings, offering a variety of recreational activities.

Recreational Therapists

Aspect	Detail
Hourly Rate	$27.5
Annual Salary	$57,200
Degree Level Required	Bachelor's degree

They plan, direct, and coordinate recreation-based treatment programs for people with disabilities, injuries, or illnesses. They use a variety of modalities, including arts and crafts, drama, music, dance, sports, and games.

Recreational Vehicle Service Technicians

Aspect	Detail
Hourly Rate	$23.1
Annual Salary	$48,000
Degree Level Required	High school diploma or equivalent

They inspect, service, and repair motorized power equipment and vehicles, especially focusing on those used for leisure activities, such as RVs and motorhomes.

Refractory Materials Repairers, Except Brickmasons

Aspect	Detail
Hourly Rate	$23.3
Annual Salary	$48,500
Degree Level Required	High school diploma or equivalent

They specialize in installing and repairing materials in furnaces, kilns, boilers, and other high-temperature structures. They work with materials that are resistant to degradation by heat.

Refuse and Recyclable Material Collectors

Aspect	Detail
Hourly Rate	$22
Annual Salary	$45,800
Degree Level Required	No formal educational credential

They collect and dump refuse or recyclable materials from containers into trucks. They play a crucial role in waste management and recycling processes.

Registered Nurses

Aspect	Detail
Hourly Rate	$41.4
Annual Salary	$86,100
Degree Level Required	Bachelor's degree

They provide and coordinate patient care, educate patients and the public about various health conditions, and provide advice and emotional support to patients and their family members.

Rehabilitation Counselors

Aspect	Detail
Hourly Rate	$21.2
Annual Salary	$44,100
Degree Level Required	Master's degree

They help people with physical, mental, developmental, or emotional disabilities live independently. They work with clients to overcome or manage the personal, social, or psychological effects of disabilities on employment or independent living.

Reinforcing Iron and Rebar Workers

Aspect	Detail
Hourly Rate	$26.4
Annual Salary	$54,900
Degree Level Required	High school diploma or equivalent

They use iron or steel bars to reinforce concrete buildings and structures. They cut, bend, and place rebar according to construction plans and specifications.

Reservation and Transportation Ticket Agents and Travel Clerks

Aspect	Detail
Hourly Rate	$19.6
Annual Salary	$40,700
Degree Level Required	High school diploma or equivalent

They make and confirm reservations for transportation or accommodations, or sell tickets for transportation agencies such as airlines, bus companies, railroads, and steamship lines.

Residential Advisors

Aspect	Detail
Hourly Rate	$18.3
Annual Salary	$38,000
Degree Level Required	High school diploma or equivalent

They coordinate activities in residential facilities in secondary and postsecondary institutions, such as dormitories, group homes, or camps. They provide support, supervision, and advice to residents.

Respiratory Therapists

Aspect	Detail
Hourly Rate	$37.5
Annual Salary	$78,000
Degree Level Required	Associate's degree

They care for patients who have trouble breathing—for example, from a chronic respiratory disease, such as asthma or emphysema. They provide emergency care to patients suffering from heart attacks, drowning, or shock.

Retail Salespersons

Aspect	Detail
Hourly Rate	$16.2
Annual Salary	$33,700
Degree Level Required	No formal educational credential

They sell merchandise, such as clothing, furniture, and automobiles. They help customers find the products they want, process customer payments, and may also handle merchandise returns and exchanges.

Riggers

Aspect	Detail
Hourly Rate	$27.1
Annual Salary	$56,300
Degree Level Required	High school diploma or equivalent

They set up and repair rigging for construction projects, manufacturing plants, logging operations, or for the entertainment industry. They ensure that the machinery, materials, and equipment are safely anchored and supported.

Rock Splitters, Quarry

Aspect	Detail
Hourly Rate	$22.4
Annual Salary	$46,600
Degree Level Required	No formal educational credential

They use specialized tools and techniques to break down large blocks of rock into smaller, more manageable pieces. They may use wedges, jackhammers, explosives, or other methods depending on the type of rock and quarry operation.

Rolling Machine Setters, Operators, and Tenders, Metal and Plastic

Aspect	Detail
Hourly Rate	$22.6
Annual Salary	$47,100
Degree Level Required	High school diploma or equivalent

They set up, operate, or tend to machines that roll metal or plastic into sheets, bars, or other shapes. They adjust machine settings, feed material into the rollers, monitor the rolling process, and ensure the quality of the output.

Roof Bolters, Mining

Aspect	Detail
Hourly Rate	$32.1
Annual Salary	$66,700
Degree Level Required	High school diploma or equivalent

They install support bolts in the roofs of mine tunnels to prevent collapses. They operate specialized drilling equipment to create holes and secure the roof bolts, ensuring the safety of the underground work environment.

Roofers

Aspect	Detail
Hourly Rate	$24.1
Annual Salary	$50,100
Degree Level Required	No formal educational credential

They install, repair, and replace roofs on buildings. They apply layers of roofing materials like shingles, asphalt, metal, or tile to protect structures from the elements.

Rotary Drill Operators, Oil and Gas

Aspect	Detail
Hourly Rate	$29.7
Annual Salary	$61,800
Degree Level Required	No formal educational credential

They control rotary drilling rigs used to drill wells for oil and gas extraction. They manage the drilling process, monitor equipment, and supervise the drilling crew.

Roustabouts, Oil and Gas

Aspect	Detail
Hourly Rate	$22.3
Annual Salary	$46,400
Degree Level Required	No formal educational credential

They perform general labor tasks on oil and gas rigs. Their work involves assembling and disassembling drilling equipment, maintaining machinery, moving materials, and assisting other rig workers as needed.

Sailors and Marine Oilers

Aspect	Detail
Hourly Rate	$23.3
Annual Salary	$48,400
Degree Level Required	No formal educational credential

They perform various tasks on ships and other water vessels. They handle lines, assist with navigation, maintain the vessel, and perform watch duty. Marine oilers maintain and repair ship engines and mechanical equipment.

Sales Engineers

Aspect	Detail
Hourly Rate	$56.3
Annual Salary	$117,000
Degree Level Required	Bachelor's degree

They sell complex scientific or technical products and services. They have technical expertise and sales skills to explain the features and benefits of their products to potential clients, often engineers or other technical professionals.

Sales Managers

Aspect	Detail
Hourly Rate	$65.0
Annual Salary	$135,200
Degree Level Required	Bachelor's degree

They oversee sales teams and develop strategies to achieve sales targets. They set sales goals, manage budgets, recruit and train sales representatives, and analyze sales data to improve performance.

Sales Representatives of Services

Aspect	Detail
Hourly Rate	$31.1
Annual Salary	$64,600
Degree Level Required	High school diploma or equivalent

They sell services rather than physical goods. They work in industries like insurance, advertising, software, or telecommunications, promoting intangible products to customers.

Sales Representatives, Wholesale and Manufacturing

Aspect	Detail
Hourly Rate	$31.6
Annual Salary	$65,700
Degree Level Required	High school diploma or equivalent

They sell goods for wholesalers or manufacturers to businesses, government agencies, or other organizations. They build relationships with clients, understand their needs, and promote their company's products.

Sawing Machine Setters, Operators, and Tenders, Wood

Aspect	Detail
Hourly Rate	$18.3
Annual Salary	$38,000
Degree Level Required	High school diploma or equivalent

They set up, operate, or tend to machines that cut wood into specific shapes and sizes. They work in sawmills or other wood processing facilities, producing lumber, wood components for furniture, or other wood products.

School Bus Monitors

Aspect	Detail
Hourly Rate	$16.0
Annual Salary	$33,200
Degree Level Required	High school diploma or equivalent

They ride on school buses to ensure the safety of students. They supervise student behavior, help students with disabilities, and may assist the bus driver if needed.

School Psychologists

Aspect	Detail
Hourly Rate	$40.9
Annual Salary	$85,000
Degree Level Required	Master's degree

They work within educational institutions to help children deal with emotional, academic, and social problems by conducting tests, providing counseling, and developing strategies to improve student success.

Secretaries and Administrative Assistants, Except Legal, Medical, and Executive

Aspect	Detail
Hourly Rate	$21.3
Annual Salary	$44,300
Degree Level Required	High school diploma or equivalent

They perform clerical and administrative duties such as filing, drafting correspondence, organizing files, and providing general support to other staff members.

Securities, Commodities, and Financial Services Sales Agents

Aspect	Detail
Hourly Rate	$37.0
Annual Salary	$76,900
Degree Level Required	Bachelor's degree

They buy and sell securities or commodities in investment and trading firms, or sell financial services to businesses and individuals. They advise clients on the stock market and manage portfolios.

Security and Fire Alarm Systems Installers

Aspect	Detail
Hourly Rate	$27.2
Annual Salary	$56,500
Degree Level Required	High school diploma or equivalent

They install, program, maintain, and repair security and fire alarm wiring and equipment. They ensure that these systems function correctly to protect individuals and property from fire and intrusions.

Security Guards

Aspect	Detail
Hourly Rate	$17.8
Annual Salary	$37,100
Degree Level Required	High school diploma or equivalent

They patrol and inspect property against theft, vandalism, terrorism, and illegal activity. They monitor entrances and exits and authorize entry, as well as report any irregularities and ensure the safety of occupants.

Semiconductor Processing Technicians

Aspect	Detail
Hourly Rate	$22.1
Annual Salary	$45,900
Degree Level Required	High school diploma or equivalent

They operate specialized equipment to manufacture semiconductor devices, such as integrated circuits found in electronic devices. They monitor and adjust production processes and clean and maintain equipment.

Septic Tank Servicers and Sewer Pipe Cleaners

Aspect	Detail
Hourly Rate	$22.6
Annual Salary	$47,000
Degree Level Required	High school diploma or equivalent

They clean and repair septic tanks, sewer lines, or drains. They may use trucks equipped with suction pumps or other equipment to remove sewage and ensure proper sanitation.

Service Unit Operators, Oil and Gas

Aspect	Detail
Hourly Rate	$26.8
Annual Salary	$55,800
Degree Level Required	No formal educational credential

They operate equipment to increase oil flow from producing wells or to remove stuck pipe, casing, tools, or other obstructions from drilling wells. They are part of the oil extraction and maintenance team.

Set and Exhibit Designers

Aspect	Detail
Hourly Rate	$28.6
Annual Salary	$59,500
Degree Level Required	Bachelor's degree

They design and plan the construction of sets for movie, television, and theater productions, and create layouts for exhibits and displays. They work closely with directors and event planners to create the desired atmosphere.

Sewers, Hand

Aspect	Detail
Hourly Rate	$15.5
Annual Salary	$32,300
Degree Level Required	No formal educational credential

They sew, join, reinforce, or finish, usually with needle and thread, a variety of manufactured items. This includes garment or non-garment products such as shoes and leather goods.

Sewing Machine Operators

Aspect	Detail
Hourly Rate	$16.6
Annual Salary	$34,500
Degree Level Required	No formal educational credential

They operate or tend sewing machines to join, reinforce, decorate, or perform related sewing operations in the manufacture of garment or non-garment products.

Shampooers

Aspect	Detail
Hourly Rate	$14.2
Annual Salary	$29,600
Degree Level Required	No formal educational credential

They clean customers' hair before haircuts or styling by applying shampoo and conditioner, and may also provide scalp massages to customers in salons or barbershops.

Sheet Metal Workers

Aspect	Detail
Hourly Rate	$28.3
Annual Salary	$58,800
Degree Level Required	High school diploma or equivalent

They fabricate, install, and maintain thin metal sheets used in a variety of applications, including HVAC ducts, metal roofing, and siding. They work in construction and manufacturing settings.

Ship Engineers

Aspect	Detail
Hourly Rate	$45.3
Annual Salary	$94,300
Degree Level Required	Postsecondary non-degree award

They operate and maintain a vessel's propulsion system, which includes the engine, boilers, generators, pumps, and other machinery. They oversee the mechanical aspects onboard to ensure the ship's operations run smoothly.

Shipping, Receiving, and Inventory Clerks

Aspect	Detail
Hourly Rate	$19.1
Annual Salary	$39,800
Degree Level Required	High school diploma or equivalent

They verify, receive, and record incoming shipments and outgoing shipments. They prepare items for shipping, maintain inventory records, and address discrepancies in orders or stock levels.

Shoe and Leather Workers and Repairers

Aspect	Detail
Hourly Rate	$17.4
Annual Salary	$36,100
Degree Level Required	High school diploma or equivalent

They create or repair shoes, boots, and other leather goods. They may work in factories assembling footwear or in repair shops, fixing damaged shoes and leather products.

Shoe Machine Operators and Tenders

Aspect	Detail
Hourly Rate	$17.8
Annual Salary	$37,000
Degree Level Required	High school diploma or equivalent

They operate or tend to various machines used in the manufacturing of shoes. They may operate cutting machines, sewing machines, lasting machines, or other specialized footwear production equipment.

Shuttle Drivers and Chauffeurs

Aspect	Detail
Hourly Rate	$17.0
Annual Salary	$35,300
Degree Level Required	No formal educational credential

They transport passengers between locations on a regular schedule, often for hotels, airports, or other venues. Chauffeurs operate private vehicles for individuals or organizations offering a more personalized transportation service.

Signal and Track Switch Repairers

Aspect	Detail
Hourly Rate	$39.8
Annual Salary	$82,800
Degree Level Required	High school diploma or equivalent

They maintain and repair railroad signaling systems and track switches, ensuring they function correctly to direct train traffic safely. They work with electrical systems and mechanical components.

Skincare Specialists

Aspect	Detail
Hourly Rate	$20.8
Annual Salary	$43,200
Degree Level Required	Postsecondary non-degree award

They they provide skincare treatments such as facials, hair removal, and apply makeup. They assess skin condition, recommend treatments and products, and perform procedures to improve the appearance of skin.

Slaughterers and Meat Packers

Aspect	Detail
Hourly Rate	$18.4
Annual Salary	$38,200
Degree Level Required	No formal educational credential

They perform the slaughtering, cleaning, and processing of livestock for meat production in slaughterhouses and meatpacking plants. Their tasks are physically demanding and follow strict safety regulations.

Social and Community Service Managers

Aspect	Detail
Hourly Rate	$37.1
Annual Salary	$77,100
Degree Level Required	Bachelor's degree

They oversee programs that provide social services or community support. They hire staff, develop programs, manage budgets, and ensure their organizations are meeting the needs of their target populations.

Social and Human Service Assistants

Aspect	Detail
Hourly Rate	$20.0
Annual Salary	$41,500
Degree Level Required	High school diploma or equivalent

They provide support to clients of social service programs, helping them access resources, connecting them with services, and assisting them with day-to-day needs.

Social Science Research Assistants

Aspect	Detail
Hourly Rate	$27.1
Annual Salary	$56,400
Degree Level Required	Bachelor's degree

They assist social scientists like sociologists, economists, or political scientists with their research projects. They may collect data, conduct interviews, analyze information, and help prepare reports.

Sociologists

Aspect	Detail
Hourly Rate	$48.9
Annual Salary	$101,800
Degree Level Required	Master's degree

They study society, social structures, social groups, and social institutions. They conduct research using various methods to analyze how factors like culture, race, gender, and class affect individuals and groups.

Software Developers

Aspect	Detail
Hourly Rate	$63.6
Annual Salary	$132,300
Degree Level Required	Bachelor's degree

They design, create, and test computer software applications. They write code, debug and troubleshoot issues, and may collaborate with other developers and designers on larger projects.

Software Quality Assurance Analysts and Testers

Aspect	Detail
Hourly Rate	$48.9
Annual Salary	$101,800
Degree Level Required	Bachelor's degree

They play a crucial role in the development process by ensuring that software applications function correctly and meet specified requirements. They conduct automated and manual tests to identify software bugs and issues.

Soil and Plant Scientists

Aspect	Detail
Hourly Rate	$32.8
Annual Salary	$68,300
Degree Level Required	Bachelor's degree

They study the composition, structure, and other physical aspects of the Earth, as well as how plants grow in different soil conditions. Their work can inform agricultural practices, help with environmental conservation, and support land management decisions.

Solar Photovoltaic Installers

Aspect	Detail
Hourly Rate	$23.5
Annual Salary	$48,800
Degree Level Required	High school diploma or equivalent

They specialize in installing and maintaining solar panel systems on rooftops or other structures to convert sunlight into electricity. They are knowledgeable about solar panel technology, electrical systems, and safety standards.

Sound Engineering Technicians

Aspect	Detail
Hourly Rate	$28.6
Annual Salary	$59,500
Degree Level Required	Postsecondary non-degree award

They operate equipment to record, synchronize, mix, or reproduce music, voices, or sound effects in recording studios, sporting arenas, theater productions, or movie and video productions.

Special Effects Artists and Animators

Aspect	Detail
Hourly Rate	$47.57
Annual Salary	$99,000
Degree Level Required	Bachelor's degree

They create visual effects and animations for movies, television, video games, and other forms of media using software and other techniques to bring life to their creations.

Speech-Language Pathologists

Aspect	Detail
Hourly Rate	$42.9
Annual Salary	$89,300
Degree Level Required	Master's degree

They assess, diagnose, treat, and help to prevent communication and swallowing disorders in children and adults. They work in a variety of settings, including schools, hospitals, and private practice.

Stationary Engineers and Boiler Operators

Aspect	Detail
Hourly Rate	$32.5
Annual Salary	$67,700
Degree Level Required	High school diploma or equivalent

They control stationary engines, boilers, or other mechanical equipment to provide utilities for buildings or industrial processes. They operate equipment such as steam engines, generators, and air-conditioning systems.

Statistical Assistants

Aspect	Detail
Hourly Rate	$24.3
Annual Salary	$50,600
Degree Level Required	Bachelor's degree

They support statisticians and other data analysts by performing tasks such as data entry, cleaning, and preliminary analysis. They help prepare reports and ensure data accuracy.

Statisticians

Aspect	Detail
Hourly Rate	$50.1
Annual Salary	$104,200
Degree Level Required	Master's degree

They apply mathematical and statistical techniques to analyze data and solve problems in various fields, including business, engineering, healthcare, or government. They design surveys, experiments, and polls to collect data, analyze it, and interpret the results.

Stockers and Order Fillers

Aspect	Detail
Hourly Rate	$17.5
Annual Salary	$36,400
Degree Level Required	High school diploma or equivalent

They receive, unpack, and track merchandise, and fill customer orders from stock. They work in warehouses, stockrooms, and stores, ensuring that products are available and shelves are stocked.

245

Stonemasons

Aspect	Detail
Hourly Rate	$25.0
Annual Salary	$51,900
Degree Level Required	High school diploma or equivalent

They cut and shape stone using various tools, creating structures or monuments. They may work on construction projects, restoring historic buildings, or crafting stonework for landscapes.

Structural Iron and Steel Workers

Aspect	Detail
Hourly Rate	$30.2
Annual Salary	$62,800
Degree Level Required	High school diploma or equivalent

They erect and assemble structural frameworks for buildings, bridges, and other structures using iron and steel beams. They work at heights and are skilled in using tools and machinery for installation.

Structural Metal Fabricators and Fitters

Aspect	Detail
Hourly Rate	$23.3
Annual Salary	$48,500
Degree Level Required	High school diploma or equivalent

They fabricate, position, align, and fit parts of structural metal products. They read blueprints and use machinery and tools to weld or bolt metal components into final products or structures.

Substance Abuse, Behavioral Disorder, and Mental Health Counselors

Aspect	Detail
Hourly Rate	$25.9
Annual Salary	$53,800
Degree Level Required	Bachelor's degree

They provide treatment and advise people who suffer from alcoholism, drug addiction, or other mental or behavioral problems. They support recovery and help clients modify behaviors.

Subway and Streetcar Operators

Aspect	Detail
Hourly Rate	$40.5
Annual Salary	$84,300
Degree Level Required	High school diploma or equivalent

They control subway trains or streetcars to transport passengers through urban areas, following schedules, and adhering to safety protocols. They manage the operation of the vehicle and ensure passenger safety.

Surgical Assistants

Aspect	Detail
Hourly Rate	$28.5
Annual Salary	$59,200
Degree Level Required	Postsecondary non-degree award

They work directly with surgeons during operations. They help prepare the operating room, handle instruments, retract tissue, and assist the surgeon as needed to ensure a smooth procedure.

Surgical Technologists

Aspect	Detail
Hourly Rate	$29.2
Annual Salary	$60,700
Degree Level Required	Postsecondary non-degree award

They prepare the operating room, sterilize instruments, assist surgeons during procedures, and handle surgical equipment. They are an integral part of the surgical team.

Survey Researchers

Aspect	Detail
Hourly Rate	$29.3
Annual Salary	$61,000
Degree Level Required	Master's degree

They design and conduct surveys to collect data on public opinion, consumer preferences, or other social trends. They develop questionnaires, analyze survey results, and report findings.

Surveying and Mapping Technicians

Aspect	Detail
Hourly Rate	$23.6
Annual Salary	$49,000
Degree Level Required	High school diploma or equivalent

They assist surveyors and cartographers. They collect geospatial data in the field using specialized equipment, perform calculations, and create maps and geographic representations.

Surveyors

Aspect	Detail
Hourly Rate	$33.0
Annual Salary	$68,600
Degree Level Required	Bachelor's degree

They measure and map the Earth's surface to determine property boundaries, provide data for construction projects, or aid in map creation. They use specialized equipment and apply mathematical techniques.

Switchboard Operators, Including Answering Service

Aspect	Detail
Hourly Rate	$17.7
Annual Salary	$36,800
Degree Level Required	High school diploma or equivalent

They manage telephone switchboard systems, routing calls and providing information. Answering service operators answer phone calls for businesses and handle messages or requests according to instructions.

Tailors, Dressmakers, and Custom Sewers

Aspect	Detail
Hourly Rate	$17.6
Annual Salary	$36,700
Degree Level Required	No formal educational credential

They design, create, alter, and repair garments. Tailors often specialize in menswear, dressmakers in women's clothing, and custom sewers create unique garments according to client specifications.

Tank Car, Truck, and Ship Loaders

Aspect	Detail
Hourly Rate	$28.2
Annual Salary	$58,700
Degree Level Required	No formal educational credential

They load and unload liquid or loose bulk materials like oil, chemicals, grain, or coal into tanker trucks, ships, or railcars. They operate pumps, monitor the loading process, and ensure safety procedures.

Tapers

Aspect	Detail
Hourly Rate	$30.5
Annual Salary	$63,400
Degree Level Required	No formal educational credential

They finish drywall joints, applying joint tape and compound to create smooth, even surfaces ready for painting.

Tax Examiners and Collectors, and Revenue Agents

Aspect	Detail
Hourly Rate	$28.2
Annual Salary	$58,600
Degree Level Required	Bachelor's degree

They ensure individuals and businesses comply with tax laws. Examiners audit tax returns, collectors work to collect overdue taxes, and revenue agents investigate complex tax-related issues.

Tax Preparers

Aspect	Detail
Hourly Rate	$23.6
Annual Salary	$49,100
Degree Level Required	High school diploma or equivalent

They help individuals and businesses file their tax returns. They calculate taxes owed, prepare the necessary forms, and ensure compliance with tax regulations.

Taxi Drivers

Aspect	Detail
Hourly Rate	$16.7
Annual Salary	$34,700
Degree Level Required	No formal educational credential

They transport passengers to their destinations in cabs. They must have knowledge of city streets, utilize navigation tools, and safely operate their vehicles, often in heavy traffic.

Teaching Assistants, Except Postsecondary

Aspect	Detail
Hourly Rate	$17.1
Annual Salary	$35,600
Degree Level Required	Some college, no degree

They support classroom teachers in primary and secondary schools by helping to supervise activities, provide attention to individual students, and assist with instructional tasks.

Teaching Assistants, Postsecondary

Aspect	Detail
Hourly Rate	$21.1
Annual Salary	$43,800
Degree Level Required	Bachelor's degree

They work in colleges and universities, assisting professors by grading papers, leading discussion sections, and sometimes teaching lower-level courses.

Technical Writers

Aspect	Detail
Hourly Rate	$38.5
Annual Salary	$80,100
Degree Level Required	Bachelor's degree

They specialize in creating manuals, how-to guides, and other documents that explain complex information in a clear and concise manner. They work in various fields including technology, science, and engineering.

Telecommunications Equipment Installers and Repairers

Aspect	Detail
Hourly Rate	$29.5
Annual Salary	$61,300
Degree Level Required	Postsecondary non-degree award

They set up, maintain, and repair devices that carry communications signals, such as telephone lines and Internet routers.

Telecommunications Line Installers and Repairers

Aspect	Detail
Hourly Rate	$31.1
Annual Salary	$64,700
Degree Level Required	High school diploma or equivalent

They work on the cables and lines used in telecommunications networks, including installing new lines and troubleshooting existing networks for service issues.

Telemarketers

Aspect	Detail
Hourly Rate	$16.6
Annual Salary	$34,500
Degree Level Required	No formal educational credential

They make telephone calls to potential customers to sell products or solicit donations. They use persuasive communication skills to achieve their sales or fundraising goals.

Telephone Operators

Aspect	Detail
Hourly Rate	$18.3
Annual Salary	$38,100
Degree Level Required	High school diploma or equivalent

They provide assistance to telephone users by connecting calls, assisting with directory inquiries, and offering customer service.

Tellers

Aspect	Detail
Hourly Rate	$18.1
Annual Salary	$37,700
Degree Level Required	High school diploma or equivalent

They are employed by banks and are responsible for handling customer transactions, including deposits, withdrawals, and money transfers.

Terrazzo Workers and Finishers

Aspect	Detail
Hourly Rate	$23.5
Annual Salary	$48,900
Degree Level Required	High school diploma or equivalent

They create and finish terrazzo floors, a composite flooring material made from chips of marble or other stone set in concrete and polished to a high shine.

Textile Bleaching and Dyeing Machine Operators

Aspect	Detail
Hourly Rate	$17.0
Annual Salary	$35,400
Degree Level Required	High school diploma or equivalent

They run machines used to bleach, dye, or otherwise treat textiles to change their color or add finishes. They monitor processes, ensure proper chemical applications, and maintain machinery.

Textile Cutting Machine Operators

Aspect	Detail
Hourly Rate	$17.6
Annual Salary	$36,700
Degree Level Required	High school diploma or equivalent

They use industrial cutting equipment to cut textiles according to patterns and specifications. They load fabrics onto cutting tables, operate precision cutting equipment, and ensure pieces are cut correctly for product manufacturing.

Textile Knitting and Weaving Machine Operators

Aspect	Detail
Hourly Rate	$17.9
Annual Salary	$37,200
Degree Level Required	High school diploma or equivalent

They set up, operate, and monitor machines that knit or weave yarn into fabrics. They oversee the formation of textiles, change or replace threads as needed, and troubleshoot any production issues.

Tile and Stone Setters

Aspect	Detail
Hourly Rate	$23.6
Annual Salary	$49,000
Degree Level Required	No formal educational credential

They install tile, marble, granite, or other natural stone on floors, walls, countertops, and other surfaces. They prepare surfaces, lay out tiles according to designs, apply mortar, and cut tiles to fit specific areas.

Timing Device Assemblers and Adjusters

Aspect	Detail
Hourly Rate	$23.5
Annual Salary	$48,900
Degree Level Required	High school diploma or equivalent

They assemble and calibrate the precise mechanisms found in watches, clocks, and other timing instruments. They work with tiny components, ensure timing accuracy, and perform quality control.

Tire Builders

Aspect	Detail
Hourly Rate	$26.0
Annual Salary	$54,100
Degree Level Required	High school diploma or equivalent

They operate machinery to assemble the components of tires before the vulcanization (curing) process. They layer rubber, steel belts, and other materials to form the tire structure.

Tire Repairers and Changers

Aspect	Detail
Hourly Rate	$17.2
Annual Salary	$35,800
Degree Level Required	High school diploma or equivalent

They repair punctures in tires, patch leaks, replace damaged tires, and balance wheels. They use specialized tools to dismount tires, make repairs, remount tires, and ensure proper inflation.

Title Examiners, Abstractors, and Searchers

Aspect	Detail
Hourly Rate	$25.8
Annual Salary	$53,600
Degree Level Required	High school diploma or equivalent

They research real estate records to ensure that a property's title is clear and ready for transfer. Examiners verify ownership, searchers gather relevant documents, and abstractors summarize the property's title history.

Tool and Die Makers

Aspect	Detail
Hourly Rate	$29.6
Annual Salary	$61,500
Degree Level Required	Postsecondary non-degree award

They create the tools, dies, molds, and jigs used in manufacturing processes. They machine precision parts from metal using a wide array of industrial tools and follow complex engineering blueprints.

Tool Grinders, Filers, and Sharpeners

Aspect	Detail
Hourly Rate	$22.4
Annual Salary	$46,500
Degree Level Required	High school diploma or equivalent

They sharpen precision cutting tools, hand tools, or other bladed implements. They use grinding machines, files, and other specialized equipment to shape and maintain sharp cutting edges.

Tour and Travel Guides

Aspect	Detail
Hourly Rate	$17.4
Annual Salary	$36,100
Degree Level Required	High school diploma or equivalent

They lead individuals and groups on tours, providing information about historical, cultural, or natural significance sites and managing logistics of the tour.

Traffic Technicians

Aspect	Detail
Hourly Rate	$25.1
Annual Salary	$52,300
Degree Level Required	High school diploma or equivalent

They work under the direction of civil engineers to develop and implement traffic control systems to ease congestion and ensure safe road conditions.

Training and Development Specialists

Aspect	Detail
Hourly Rate	$31.0
Annual Salary	$64,400
Degree Level Required	Bachelor's degree

They design, deliver, and evaluate employee training programs. They assess training needs, develop instructional materials, conduct training sessions, and measure the effectiveness of training initiatives.

Transit and Railroad Police

Aspect	Detail
Hourly Rate	$34.8
Annual Salary	$72,300
Degree Level Required	High school diploma or equivalent

They patrol public transportation systems like subways, buses, and trains, as well as railroad property. They enforce laws, deter crime, respond to emergencies, and ensure the safety of passengers and railway operations.

Transportation Inspectors

Aspect	Detail
Hourly Rate	$42.0
Annual Salary	$87,300
Degree Level Required	High school diploma or equivalent

They ensure compliance with regulations and safety standards in various transportation industries. They may inspect aircraft, commercial vehicles, railroads, or cargo, verifying maintenance, operation, and security procedures are followed.

Transportation Security Screeners

Aspect	Detail
Hourly Rate	$24.1
Annual Salary	$50,100
Degree Level Required	High school diploma or equivalent

They work for organizations like the TSA, operating security checkpoints at airports, train stations, or other transportation hubs. They screen passengers, luggage, and cargo, utilizing X-ray machines, metal detectors, and other screening tools.

Transportation, Storage, and Distribution Managers

Aspect	Detail
Hourly Rate	$47.7
Annual Salary	$99,200
Degree Level Required	High school diploma or equivalent

They coordinate activities related to transportation, warehousing, and the distribution of goods. They optimize logistics networks, manage fleets, negotiate shipping contracts, and oversee inventory management to ensure efficient and cost-effective operations.

Travel Agents

Aspect	Detail
Hourly Rate	$22.8
Annual Salary	$47,500
Degree Level Required	High school diploma or equivalent

They help individuals and groups plan and book travel arrangements. They research destinations, make reservations for flights, hotels, and tours, suggest itineraries, and handle travel documents.

Tree Trimmers and Pruners

Aspect	Detail
Hourly Rate	$23.6
Annual Salary	$49,100
Degree Level Required	High school diploma or equivalent

They maintain the health and appearance of trees and shrubs. They remove dead or excess branches, shape trees, and may assess trees for disease or safety hazards.

Tutors

Aspect	Detail
Hourly Rate	$19.0
Annual Salary	$39,600
Degree Level Required	Some college, no degree

They provide individualized academic support to students outside of the traditional classroom setting. They reinforce concepts taught in school, address learning difficulties, and help students develop study skills.

Umpires, Referees, and Other Sports Officials

Aspect	Detail
Hourly Rate	$17.3
Annual Salary	$35,900
Degree Level Required	High school diploma or equivalent

They preside over sporting events, enforcing the rules of the game, making fair judgments, ensuring athlete safety, and keeping score. They need a deep understanding of their specific sport.

Upholsterers

Aspect	Detail
Hourly Rate	$20.6
Annual Salary	$42,800
Degree Level Required	High school diploma or equivalent

They build, repair, and replace upholstery on furniture. They cut fabric, attach padding and springs, cover furniture with finished fabric, and may create custom upholstery designs.

Urban and Regional Planners

Aspect	Detail
Hourly Rate	$39.3
Annual Salary	$81,800
Degree Level Required	Master's degree

They develop long-term plans for the use of land in cities, towns, and surrounding areas. They consider factors like population growth, transportation, environmental impact, and zoning regulations to create sustainable and functional communities.

Ushers, Lobby Attendants, and Ticket Takers

Aspect	Detail
Hourly Rate	$14.3
Annual Salary	$29,800
Degree Level Required	No formal educational credential

They work at theaters, concert venues, museums, or other event spaces. They greet patrons, direct them to their seats, take tickets, check tickets, and may provide information or assistance to guests.

Veterinarians

Aspect	Detail
Hourly Rate	$57.3
Annual Salary	$119,100
Degree Level Required	Doctoral or professional degree

They provide medical care to animals. They diagnose and treat illnesses and injuries, perform surgery, administer vaccinations, and educate pet owners about preventative animal care.

Veterinary Assistants and Laboratory Animal Caretakers

Aspect	Detail
Hourly Rate	$17.5
Annual Salary	$36,500
Degree Level Required	High school diploma or equivalent

They help veterinarians and veterinary technicians by restraining animals, preparing them for procedures, cleaning cages, and performing basic care tasks. Laboratory animal caretakers feed, handle, and maintain healthy environments for animals used in research.

Veterinary Technologists and Technicians

Aspect	Detail
Hourly Rate	$21.1
Annual Salary	$43,800
Degree Level Required	Associate's degree

They carry out many of the medical tasks in veterinary clinics. They take x-rays, collect blood samples, assist in surgeries, administer medications, and provide care to animals under a veterinarian's supervision.

Waiters and Waitresses

Aspect	Detail
Hourly Rate	$15.4
Annual Salary	$32,000
Degree Level Required	No formal educational credential

They take orders, serve food and drinks, prepare customer checks, and provide a positive dining experience for restaurant patrons.

Watch and Clock Repairers

Aspect	Detail
Hourly Rate	$28.0
Annual Salary	$58,200
Degree Level Required	High school diploma or equivalent

They repair, clean, and adjust watches and clocks. They work with delicate mechanisms, diagnose issues, replace parts, and ensure timepieces function correctly.

Water and Wastewater Treatment Plant Operators

Aspect	Detail
Hourly Rate	$26.4
Annual Salary	$54,900
Degree Level Required	High school diploma or equivalent

They run equipment and manage processes at water and wastewater treatment plants to ensure clean drinking water and proper wastewater treatment. They monitor systems, adjust treatment processes, and perform equipment maintenance.

Web and Digital Interface Designers

Aspect	Detail
Hourly Rate	$47.4
Annual Salary	$98,600
Degree Level Required	Bachelor's degree

They focus on the visual layout, user experience (UX), and functionality of websites and digital applications. They blend graphic design skills with knowledge of user interaction to create intuitive and engaging online experiences.

Web Developers

Aspect	Detail
Hourly Rate	$40.9
Annual Salary	$85,000
Degree Level Required	Bachelor's degree

They build the underlying functionality of websites and web applications. They write code in languages like HTML, CSS, and JavaScript, manage databases, and ensure websites operate smoothly across different browsers and devices.

Welders, Cutters, Solderers, and Brazers

Aspect	Detail
Hourly Rate	$23.6
Annual Salary	$49,000
Degree Level Required	High school diploma or equivalent

They join or sever metal parts using high heat and various specialized processes. Welders permanently fuse metal, cutters sever metal, solderers join using a lower-temperature filler material, and brazers use a similar, higher-temperature technique.

Wellhead Pumpers

Aspect	Detail
Hourly Rate	$34.6
Annual Salary	$71,900
Degree Level Required	High school diploma or equivalent

They operate and maintain pumps that extract oil and gas from wells. They monitor well production, manage equipment, and conduct routine maintenance.

Wind Turbine Service Technicians

Aspect	Detail
Hourly Rate	$29.7
Annual Salary	$61,800
Degree Level Required	Postsecondary non-degree award

They install, inspect, maintain, and repair wind turbines. They work at heights to climb turbines, troubleshoot mechanical and electrical issues, and replace components.

Word Processors and Typists

Aspect	Detail
Hourly Rate	$22.4
Annual Salary	$46,500
Degree Level Required	High school diploma or equivalent

They input and format text documents. They transcribe from audio recordings, hand-written notes, or other sources, may edit content, and produce professional documents like letters, reports, or manuscripts.

Writers and Authors

Aspect	Detail
Hourly Rate	$35.4
Annual Salary	$73,700
Degree Level Required	Bachelor's degree

They create written content for various purposes. They may write novels, articles, poems, scripts, technical documentation, or website content, often specializing within a particular genre or field.

Zoologists and Wildlife Biologists

Aspect	Detail
Hourly Rate	$33.9
Annual Salary	$70,600
Degree Level Required	Bachelor's degree

They study animals and their interactions with ecosystems. Zoologists may focus on specific animal groups or characteristics, while wildlife biologists often research wildlife populations, habitats, and the effects of human activity on animal life.

Thank you!

We dedicated many hours to compiling this information for you. This is the book we would have loved having during our teen years and later on when we switched careers.

If you find this career guide useful, please consider leaving a review on Amazon. We'd love to hear from you!

You can use this QR code to submit your review

- "200 Jobs Explained: The Ultimate Career Guide. Discover the career of your dreams with 200 career profiles to explore"

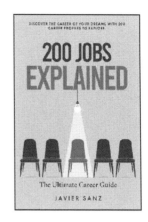

- "Famous in STEM" collection:

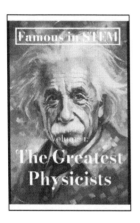  

- "Excel Tips And Tricks: Answers The Top Excel Questions On The Internet"

- **Paws and Beyond: Wild Friends in Bright Colors. Artistic Visions of the Animal Kingdom**

- **"The Motorcycle Picture Book: Amazing illustrations of all types of motorcycles"**

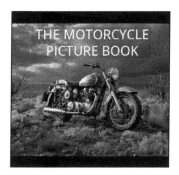